WOMEN in POLITICS

Madeleine Albright

16309

PORTSMOUTH
MIDDLE SCHOOL
LIBRARY

Women in Politics

Madeleine Albright

Benazir Bhutto

Hillary Rodham Clinton

Elizabeth Dole

Nancy Pelosi

Queen Noor

WOMEN in POLITICS

Madeleine Albright

Kerry Acker

16309

CHELSEA HOUSE
PUBLISHERS
A Haights Cross Communications Company
Philadelphia

PORTSMOUTH
MIDDLE SCHOOL
LIBRARY

CHELSEA HOUSE PUBLISHERS

VP, NEW PRODUCT DEVELOPMENT Sally Cheney
DIRECTOR OF PRODUCTION Kim Shinners
CREATIVE MANAGER Takeshi Takahashi
MANUFACTURING MANAGER Diann Grasse

Staff for MADELEINE ALBRIGHT

EXECUTIVE EDITOR Lee Marcott
ASSOCIATE EDITOR Kate Sullivan
PRODUCTION EDITOR Megan Emery
PHOTO EDITOR Sarah Bloom
SERIES & COVER DESIGNER Terry Mallon
LAYOUT 21st Century Publishing and Communications, Inc.

©2004 by Chelsea House Publishers,
a subsidiary of Haights Cross Communications.
All rights reserved. Printed and bound in the United States of America.

A Haights Cross Communications ⌖ Company

www.chelseahouse.com

First Printing

9 8 7 6 5 4 3 2 1

Library of Congress Cataloging-in-Publication Data applied for.

ISBN 0-7910-7734-9 HC   0-7910-7998-8 PB

Table of Contents

Madeleine Albright

The Highest-Ranking Woman in U.S. Government

"I never even thought about the possibility of being secretary of state before . . . because who would have ever thought that a girl who arrived from Czechoslovakia at age 11 could become secretary of state of the most powerful country in the world?"

—Madeleine Albright

When Madeleine Albright was sworn in as secretary of state on a cold winter day in January 1997, America and the rest of world watched with excitement and anticipation as history was made. No woman in U.S. history had ever held the office before. In many ways, however, it made perfect sense that Madeleine Albright had reached this point. It seemed the next logical step in her remarkable career in foreign policy. As President Bill Clinton's choice for U.S. ambassador to the United Nations, she had developed a reputation for being a tough and aggressive defender of U.S. interests. Clinton had been particularly impressed with Albright's strong, clear stance

Madeleine Albright is sworn in as secretary of state by Vice President Al Gore on January 23, 1997 as her three daughters and President Bill Clinton observe. The event, which was broadcast to millions around the world, seemed to represent the best of the American dream: Albright, who had come to the United States as an eleven-year-old Czechoslovakian refugee, was now the highest-ranking woman in the history of U.S. government.

on the civil war situation in Bosnia, where Serbs were killing innocent Muslims and forcing them to flee. Adamantly opposed to dictatorships of any kind, Albright had lobbied passionately for U.S. military intervention in the region. She had also become a visible presence in the news, known just as much for her no-nonsense, blunt style, as for her witty one-liners.

Some people felt that Albright's willingness to endorse military action seemed reckless, but others admired her and respected her stridently pro-American policies. For all the criticism leveled at her, no one could argue that Madeleine Albright did not love the United States of America. Albright, the eldest daughter of a Czechoslovakian diplomat, had come to the United States as an eleven-year-old refugee. She and her family had been forced to flee her native country twice—first to escape the Nazis and, after returning, to escape communism. The freedom that she and her family finally found in the United States endowed her with a passionate and deep appreciation for the democratic values for which America stands. Her own history, and that of her family, played a tremendous role in shaping the political ideals that would characterize her illustrious career.

A childhood spent in Belgrade, London, and Switzerland gave young Madeleine a solid grasp of the Czech, English, and French languages as well as a distinct talent for adapting and thriving in any situation. Although Albright would always feel like an outsider in some ways, she developed an uncanny ability to relate to and connect with different types of people.

When her family arrived in the United States, Albright studied at an elite private school in Colorado, where she distinguished herself from her classmates with her love of foreign policy, organizational skills, and sense of fun. After she graduated from Wellesley College, Albright married the heir to a vast newspaper fortune, Joseph Medill Albright. While raising her three children, at a time when most women were not encouraged to pursue their own careers, Madeleine Albright managed to earn a doctorate. She went on to become one of the Democratic Party's foremost foreign policy experts. By the time President Bill Clinton was elected in 1993, Albright had worked for the Carter administration and had served as an advisor to Democratic candidates Geraldine Ferraro and Michael Dukakis. She had won awards for her teaching at the Georgetown University School of Foreign Service, served as president for the Center for National Policy, and firmly established her formidable presence in the realm of international affairs. She had also raised three smart and lively young women.

After serving as U.S. ambassador to the United Nations during President Clinton's first term in office, Albright was selected by Clinton to be the first female secretary of state, the president's main advisor on foreign policy and the highest U.S. government position ever held by a woman. The Senate approved her in a unanimous vote.

Madeleine Albright's love for foreign policy began at a very young age, and much of what she believes is rooted in the history of her family, especially in the experiences of her father, Josef Korbel. Her story begins long ago in Prague, the cosmopolitan capital of Czechoslovakia, the Bohemian land whose rich and complicated past can be closely linked to Madeleine Albright's own vibrant yet painful family history.

Czechoslovakia

1878–1937

"To be a Jew is to be constantly threatened by some kind of danger. That is our history."

—Mandula Albright, Madeleine's mother

For centuries, Prague was one of the most significant Jewish centers in all of Europe. Jews have lived in the kingdom of Bohemia and Moravia (which later became parts of Czechoslovakia) since the ninth century, when Jewish trade caravans in the hills and valleys around the city dealt in such wares as grain, exotic spices, wool, tin, horses, and cattle. Yet for as long as they lived in the region, and in Europe as a whole, Jewish families were the targets of hatred and prejudice. In the eleventh century, Crusaders launched violent attacks against the Jews; those who survived were forced to convert to Christianity. By the early thirteenth century, Jews were declared slaves of the Holy Roman Empire and lost many of their rights. The pope decreed that Jews were to be separated from Christians, and a wall was built around the Jewish quarter of Prague. In the fourteenth century, Jews in Prague were victims of a vicious pogrom, a bloody and organized massacre directed against those of Jewish heritage. Claiming that Jews had desecrated the Holy Eucharist, members of the Christian clergy encouraged citizens to ransack and burn the Jewish quarter. In the fifteenth century, Jews were banished from all royal towns in Moravia.

Despite this relentless persecution, the Jewish community in Bohemia was flourishing intellectually, spiritually, and culturally by the late sixteenth and early seventeenth centuries. During this period, known as the Golden Age of Prague, Jews were granted some economic freedom, and a great number of them became successful businessmen. Others became scientists, historians, philosophers, and artists. In 1781, the Hapsburg (the Austrian dynasty that ruled over Bohemia from 1526 to 1918) emperor, Joseph II, declared that Jewish people were "almost equal" to Christians. This "almost equality" came at a high price. Jews would have to stop speaking their traditional language, Yiddish, and instead speak German, the official language of the empire. They would have to be educated in Christian-run schools and wear Christian-style clothing. (The Hapsburgs had instituted an empire-wide policy of Germanization. Under this policy, both Christian and Jewish Czechs were marginalized.) It wasn't until the mid-nineteenth century that Jews regained their full civil and political rights. Thus began another period of intellectual and creative growth in Jewish Bohemia. The era produced such prominent Jewish figures as the writer Franz Kafka, the composer Gustav Mahler, and the founder of psychoanalysis, Sigmund Freud.

By the end of nineteenth century, there were 95,000 Jews

in Bohemia and 45,000 in Moravia. Yet it was a strange time for Jews in the region. There was a broad movement within the Czech and Slovak communities to assert independence from their Hapsburg rulers and establish a separate national identity. Many Jews were torn; they struggled to find ways to get along with both their Czech neighbors and their Hapsburg rulers.

Madeleine Albright's paternal grandfather, Arnost Körbel, was born on June 7, 1878 in the midst of this turbulent time. Living in the village of Kuncice, an old farming community located about ninety miles east of Prague, he and his brothers and sisters all followed their father Josef into the railroad business as it expanded across the beautiful Bohemian countryside. Josef's sons, including Arnost, worked for the Austrian North-Western Railroad Company, and his daughters married men who worked for the company.

While Arnost was working for the railroad in Novy Bydzov, he met Olga Ptackova, a girl from a nearby town called Kostelec. They married and settled in Kysperk, in the Czech-speaking part of the country. Like many other Jews of that time, Arnost was a secular Jew. He observed only basic Jewish rituals and holidays, and he celebrated Christian holidays with the community. Most villagers didn't realize he was Jewish. He even refused to allow Olga to attend synagogue, but she occasionally went to services in secret. (It bears noting that anti-Semitism was particularly virulent around this time. In 1897 a three-day pogrom occurred in Prague. Synagogues and Jewish-owned businesses were burned and looted and Jews were assaulted; many were killed. The attacks stopped only when the government called in troops. Two years after that an entire Jewish town—Polna— was accused of murdering a Christian woman. Another pogrom ensued.) Yet when Arnost's father Josef died in 1906, in an area with few Jewish residents and no Jewish cemetery,

Arnost brought the body to be buried in the Jewish cemetery in Novy Bydzov.

Arnost's desire to assimilate wasn't unusual for Jews of the era. He eventually switched from the railroad industry to the building materials trade—a field that was traditionally not welcoming to Jews. Arnost worked hard and soon became the comanager of a successful building materials business. He used the ground floor of his home, a rowhouse situated across the street from the Kysperk railroad station, as a business office. The sign advertising the goods he sold was written in Czech, as opposed to Hebrew, one indication that the family had totally assimilated into Czech society.

Arnost was also responsible for supplying wood to a nearby match factory. He transported the timber into town by rail and then used his horses to carry the logs to the factory. Neighbors and business associates remembered Arnost as a determined, charismatic, and generous man. He seemed to possess both ambition and a gift for understanding people (a potent combination of traits that his son Josef and granddaughter Madeleine appear to have inherited), and he grew quite prosperous. Relatives and friends described Olga as a compassionate and unselfish woman.

Arnost and Olga's oldest child was a daughter named Margareta (born in 1903), who eventually married a doctor. Jan, their second child (born in 1906), went into the family business. Their last son, Josef (born in 1909), was Madeleine Albright's father. Josef was driven and ambitious, even in childhood. His life experiences and beliefs played a prodigious role in shaping his daughter's own ideals and sensibilities.

JOSEF AND MANDULA

Josef Körbel was born on September 20, 1909. His birth certificate was stamped "Jewish and legitimate." Like his two siblings, he was raised as a Czech, but Arnost and Olga also taught all their children to speak fluent German. The Körbels placed great emphasis on the children's education, and Josef performed very well academically.

When Josef was about nine years old, he witnessed some major historical events that would affect him for the rest of his life. The end of World War I in 1918 signaled the demise of the Hapsburg Empire and the beginning of democracy for Czechs and Slovaks. Their long-held desire for freedom had become a reality. Centuries of Austro-Hungarian authoritarian rule had finally come to an end and the Czechs and Slovaks united to form an independent state. On October 28, 1918, the Republic of Czechoslovakia was born, and the people soon elected Tomás Masaryk as their first president. The Körbels

TOMÁS MASARYK

Tomás Masaryk (1850–1937), "the father of Czechoslovakia," was a true role model for young Josef Korbel. Born in Moravia (then part of the Austro-Hungarian Empire), Masaryk studied in Brno, Leipzig, and Vienna, before becoming a professor at the Czech University in Prague. Before the war, Masaryk became known for his opposition to racial prejudice and his agitation for the creation of an independent Czech state. When World War I broke out, he avoided arrest and fled to Geneva and London, where he advocated tirelessly for Czech independence. As the Austro-Hungarian Empire disintegrated, the Allied countries recognized him as the head of the temporary Czech government, and he was officially elected president in 1920. Masaryk was an ardent defender of democracy and equality among the new nation's many ethnic and religious groups, and he was quite sympathetic to Jews. Josef Korbel would be profoundly influenced by Masaryk's beliefs and politics throughout his life.

immediately embraced their new democratic state. Josef loved his new, free country, and he took great pride in being a Czechoslovakian.

When Josef was twelve years old, he was sent to a high school in Kostelec, the prosperous nearby community. He continued to do well academically, and he also participated in many school activities. From a very young age, he knew that he wanted to be a politician, a diplomat, or a journalist. It was in Kostelec that he met Anna Spiegelova, the girl that would become his wife. (Anna's formal surname was Spiegel. In Slavic languages, "ova" is added to a family name for girls and women.)

The Spiegels were one of the wealthiest families in town. Anna's maternal grandfather, Alois, had owned a successful general store, where home-roasted coffee, tea, spices, margarine, and a sweet liqueur called "Asko" (made from a family recipe) were sold. When Alois died in 1913, his two sons, Alfred and Gustav, took over the business. Alfred was remembered as a lively, talkative man. Like his granddaughter Madeleine, he had a quick wit. His wife, Ruzena, was much quieter. The Spiegels, like the Körbels, do not seem to have been very religious. They probably attended synagogue only once or twice a year. Unlike the Körbels, however, the townspeople seemed to know that the Spiegels were Jewish.

Andula, as Anna Spiegel was affectionately called by her parents, was vivacious, smart, and pretty. Josef once called her "the most talkative woman in eastern Czechoslovakia" (she promptly slapped him for this remark).[1] When she was a teenager, her parents sent her to Les Hirondelles, a finishing school in Geneva, Switzerland. There, she learned to speak French and studied secretarial skills.

Meanwhile, Josef had grown into an attractive man, full of strong opinions and burning with ambition. As Andula wrote later, "There were so many possibilities in the new

Czechoslovakia for talented young people who wanted to [take part] in building a real democracy under the leadership of T. G. M[asaryk]. . . . Joe wanted very much to be one of them."[2] He recognized that mastering other languages would be vital to a successful career in diplomacy. During vacations, he had a private tutor who taught him German. He also spent some time in the German-speaking section of Czechoslovakia to practice the language. In 1928, he went abroad to Paris, where he learned French and studied liberal arts. This was also the year that he proposed to Andula, whom he nicknamed "Mandula" ("My Little Anna"). Because their families thought that the couple was too young to get married, they waited seven more years until they finally wed.

When he returned to Prague in 1929, Josef began to attend classes at the prestigious Charles University, where he studied economics and international law. He completed his doctorate in May of 1933 and then briefly worked for a law firm in Prague. He then spent some time fulfilling his obligatory military service, during which he also learned some English and Russian. When he was just twenty-four years old, Josef joined Czechoslovakia's Ministry of Foreign Affairs.

In April 1935, after a seven-year engagement, Josef and Mandula were married in Prague. Mandula once said of their long engagement, "Joe was certainly a man worth waiting for . . . but it wasn't always easy."[3] On their marriage certificate, on the space where they were supposed to fill in their religion, they both wrote, "without denomination."[4]

By the time Josef and Mandula were married, anyone in Czechoslovakia (and in all of Europe for that matter) who was Jewish—regardless of their level of involvement in the religion and culture—had great reason to be concerned. In the neighboring country Germany, Nazi leader Adolf

Albright's parents, Josef and Mandula Körbel, became active members in the society of the intellectual elite of Czechoslovakia's capital city, Prague. Despite their high standing and Josef's important work for the government, the Körbels had to make great strides to hide their Jewish ancestry in the era in which Hitler had just come to power in Germany. Later, as Europe grew increasingly hostile toward Jews, the Körbels would rely on the connections they formed to secure the safety of Madeleine and the rest of their family.

Hitler—whose extreme racist, anti-Semitic views were outlined in his book *Mein Kampf* (1925)—had become chancellor in 1933.

THE RISE OF HITLER AND THE NAZIS

The German economy, like that of the United States, was in a state of chaos after World War I. The stock market crash of October 29, 1929, had plunged the United States and most of the rest of the world into the Great Depression. Millions of people lost their jobs, banks closed, and inflation skyrocketed. The economic crisis was particularly devastating in Germany because, according to the terms of the Treaty of Versailles signed after World War I, the nation had also to pay billions of dollars in war reparations. Thousands of hungry and out-of-work Germans lined up at soup kitchens across the country. One of the horrible effects of this misery in Germany was the rise of extremist political parties—like Hitler's National Socialists Workers' (Nazi) Party. Hitler and his radically nationalist platform appealed to the desperate and angry German populace. The country, humiliated after losing the war, responded to his forceful, clear message: a promise to restore Germany's reputation as a strong nation. Unfortunately for millions of innocent people, Hitler placed the blame for the nation's woes squarely on Jewish people and other minorities.

When German President Paul von Hindenburg died in August of 1934, Hitler swiftly named himself *Führer* ("leader") and completely abolished the presidency. He was in complete control of the German government. The rest of the world—most especially Germany's neighbors—grew increasingly uneasy.

Although some of Josef's cousins responded to the rise of Hitler and the resurgence of anti-Semitism by becoming Zionists (supporters of the creation of an independent Jewish nation), Josef, like his father before him, continued along the path of assimilation. Josef, after all, had always viewed himself as a Czechoslovakian. He also seems to have been one of the few Jews to work in the Foreign Ministry before World War II erupted.

The newlyweds first lived in an attractive art nouveau apartment in Prague, where they had lots of friends and an active social life, but in January 1937, Josef was assigned to a post in Belgrade, Yugoslavia, where he was to be a junior press attaché at the Czechoslovakian embassy. Mandula, then six months pregnant, accompanied him.

Shortly before Mandula was ready to give birth, she returned to Prague. On May 15, 1937, Marie Jana Körbelova was born. Named after Mandula's sister, Marie, the baby was nicknamed "Madla" by her grandmother. The name soon evolved into "Madlenka" and then, finally, Madeleine. On her birth certificate, where parents are supposed to identify a baby's religion, the Körbels wrote "without denomination."

The War Years

1937–1945

"If you have sacrificed my nation to preserve the peace of the world, I will be the first to applaud you. But if not, gentlemen, God help your souls."
—Jan Masaryk, Czech Minister, 1938 to the
Prime Minister of Britain in response to the Munich Pact

When baby Madlenka was old enough to make the journey, Mandula rejoined Josef in Yugoslavia. Because Belgrade was more rural than cosmopolitan Prague, it required some adjustment for the Körbels. Mandula and Josef enjoyed their new life and developed friendships with many of the city's intellectuals, artists, musicians, and writers. Mandula wrote about that time, "Because we were young and happy, we both sometimes ignored the dark clouds which were forming on the political sky around us. We were all well aware of it, but were hoping that it would somehow pass without catastrophe."[1]

HITLER INVADES CZECHOSLOVAKIA

While the young Körbel family was living relatively peacefully in seemingly tranquil Belgrade, German dictator Adolf Hitler was rapidly consolidating his power. By this time, he had firmly established a totalitarian state, the Third Reich, and all political opposition within the country was brutally suppressed. The Nazis outlawed elections, controlled the media, restricted personal liberties, and tolerated no political dissent. The Gestapo (the Nazi Party secret police) and the SS (*Schutzstaffein*, the Nazi Party militia) ruthlessly enforced this policy of intolerance, and all sectors of German society were engaged in a program called "coordination" (or *gleich-schaltung*) to support Hitler and the Nazi Party. Young persons between the ages of ten and eighteen were forced into the Hitler Youth Movement (the *Hitlerjugend*), a quasi-military organization. German Jews lost their rights of citizenship and property, and thousands of them fled the country. Jewish businesses were destroyed, and those who held positions in education or government were removed.

The Führer was also aggressively moving ahead with his plans for territorial expansion. In 1936, in defiance of the Versailles treaty, Hitler seized the Rhineland, a region in western Germany situated along the banks of the Rhine River. He allied himself with Italian dictator Benito Mussolini and Spain's Francisco Franco. After Hitler invaded Austria in early 1938, he turned his attention to Czechoslovakia, the most industrialized nation in Eastern Europe. On May 28, 1938, he said to his generals, "It is my unshakable will that Czechoslovakia be wiped off the map."[2]

Meanwhile, Josef Körbel's role model, Tomás Masaryk, had died in the fall of 1937, as the future of his democratic country was growing increasingly precarious. Eduard Beneš, Masaryk's foreign minister, had succeeded him as Czech president in 1935, and Beneš was left to grapple with the escalating crisis with Hitler that resulted in the dismemberment of Czechoslovakia.

Hitler's pretext for moving into Czechoslovakia centered on the Sudetenland, an area of western Czechoslovakia that was home to 3 million Germans. The Sudetenland had been taken from Germany after World War I, and Hitler claimed that the German minority there was being oppressed by the Czechs because the German-speakers were in solidarity with the Nazis. Hitler justified intervening in Czechoslovakia by exploiting this issue. The Czechs had made some concessions to the Sudenten Germans, but Hitler claimed that those concessions were inadequate. Although Beneš initially resisted Hitler's demands, his more powerful allies in France and Great Britain did not, and they ultimately lacked the willingness to put their countries at risk for the sake of Czechoslovakia.

On September 30, 1938, French Prime Minister Edouard Daladier, British Prime Minister Neville Chamberlain, and Italian dictator Benito Mussolini signed a pact with Germany and Italy known as the Munich Pact. Under the agreement, Czechoslovakia, which was not represented at the negotiations, was forced to hand over the Sudetenland under specific conditions. Madeleine Albright was only one year old at the time, but the ramifications of this policy of appeasement stayed with her throughout her life.

Although 800,000 Czech reservists (including Josef Körbel) had been mobilized before the agreement, and the Czechs seemed prepared to fight for their nation, Beneš knew that his country—abandoned by its western allies—couldn't face the tyrannical Hitler and his formidable Nazis alone. He and his cabinet resigned from their positions in protest. Many Czechoslovaks braced themselves for the worst.

Josef later wrote, "[In 1918], Czechoslovakia gained independence without firing a shot; twenty years later, the nation lost it without firing a shot."[3] Although he, like many others, blamed Great Britain and France for the failure at Munich, he also criticized Beneš and Masaryk for their shortcomings as leaders during the crisis:

During the critical months preceding Munich, [the] leaders had made only perfunctory remarks about national self-reliance and the country's military strength. . . . No psychological preparation had been even explored should the eventuality of facing the enemy alone ever arise.[4]

THE KÖRBELS FLEE

Two months after the signing of the Munich agreement, Josef Körbel was ordered to return to Prague from Belgrade. Beneš's supporters had assembled an "endangered persons" list of those whose lives were thought to be in jeopardy. Körbel's name made the list. Josef Körbel was not only in danger because of his political associations, but he also had reason to be afraid because of his heritage. Although the Körbels were secular Jews, the Nazi viewpoint was that anyone with even a trace of Jewish blood was considered a Jew. As Madeleine's cousin Dagmar once said, "The only sense in which we were Jews was under the definition of the Nuremberg laws, Hitler and the Nazis."[5]

There was widespread anti-Jewish sentiment in Czechoslovakia by this time—anti-Semitic publications and demonstrations were common. Many Jewish people converted to Catholicism; others committed suicide. After all, they had heard about what was happening in Germany. At the end of 1938, on *Kristallnacht,* the "night of broken glass," Jewish homes and businesses were ransacked and hundreds of synagogues were burned down. Jewish children were expelled from German schools.

Josef traveled to France and England to get in touch with people in the Czechoslovakian resistance and to use his contacts to secure a job for a Yugoslav newspaper in London. He returned to Prague on March 13, 1939, just two days before the Nazi tanks roared into the city. In an eleven-page history written thirty years after the war, Mandula Körbel described what the city was like at the time. She wrote, "To leave Czechoslovakia was technically impossible. There was complete chaos in Prague. Communications were stopped a little while, banks were closed, friends were arrested."[6]

Because of Josef's connections to Yugoslav leaders, he was able to get the necessary faked documents that enabled the family to cross the border into Yugoslavia. While waiting for their forged diplomatic papers, Josef and Mandula moved out of their apartment and walked the streets in order to avoid arrest. Little twenty-two-month-old Madlenka stayed with Mandula's mother in the countryside while her parents crouched in alleyways, hid in cafes, and slept at friends' houses, trying to stay one step ahead of the Gestapo. Mandula wrote, "With all the possible and impossible planning, and with the help of some good friends, lots of luck and a little bribery, the last plan worked."[7]

As soon as they procured the papers, Mandula and Josef retrieved baby Madlenka, quickly said their good-byes, and hustled onboard an 11:00 P.M. train headed for Belgrade. After about two weeks there, they traveled to Greece, and finally, safely reached Great Britain in May 1939. They met up with Josef's brother Jan Körbel and his family, who had fled there earlier. Mandula and Josef would never see their parents again.

LONDON

With money that Arnost Körbel had made from the sale of his building materials business, Josef, Mandula, and Madlenka were able to afford food and shelter. When they first arrived in London, the Körbels moved into a bleak boardinghouse. Josef sought out other Czech exiles and full-time employment; Mandula, who spoke no English, whiled away the hours in public parks with Madlenka.

Within a few weeks, Josef managed to get in touch with Eduard Beneš and Jan Masaryk (the son of Tomás) and other exiled colleagues. The group quickly opened an office for the Czech government in exile. Soon, the Körbel family left the boardinghouse for an eight-story apartment building located near Hyde Park, where most of their neighbors were other émigré families. Indeed, the Körbels spent most of their time in England with fellow Czech refugees.

While Jan and Josef Körbel and their families were living safely (at least for a time) in London, other members of the extended Körbel clan were scrambling to get out of Czechoslovakia. One of the lucky ones was Madlenka's first cousin Dagmar, the oldest daughter of Margareta (Josef and Jan's sister) and her husband Rudolf Deiml. Sadly, the Deimls weren't able to secure a visa in time to escape from Czechoslovakia, but they did arrange passage via the *kindertransporte* for their daughters, eleven-year-old Dagmar and her six-year-old sister Milena. (An Englishman named Nicholas Winton had managed to oversee the evacuation of 700 children from Czechoslovakia in this manner.) Two days before the girls were supposed to leave, Milena broke her arm. Although it is unclear exactly why Milena never made the voyage to Great Britain, Dagmar managed to do so.

Dagmar boarded the train to London on July 1, 1939. The young girl traveled from Prague to Holland and then took a ferry to Harwich on the coast of England. She then got on another train to London. She was met at the station by Josef Körbel, who had agreed, along with his brother Jan, to act as a sponsor for her. They enrolled Dagmar, nine years older than Madlenka, in a private school called the Berkhamsted School for Girls, where her English improved rapidly. She spent the rest of her time in England shuttling back and forth between Jan's and Josef's families.

Madlenka, meanwhile, was growing into a precocious little girl. She adapted very quickly to her surroundings and seemed exceptional even at a young age. She said years later, "I made friends very easily. I think it has to do with the fact that I lived in a lot of different countries, went to a lot of different schools and was always being put into situations where I had to relate to the people around me."[8] A colleague of Josef Körbel's said of the young Madlenka, "I remember her as everywhere, terribly intelligent, a doer. Madlenka had to be noticed."[9]

By this time, Josef was heading up the Czech information department. He was working closely with both Jan Masaryk (who became the foreign minister of the Czech government in exile) and Eduard Beneš, both of whom held Josef in high regard. Josef was known for his professionalism and efficiency, and he was greatly respected for his work, which eventually included broadcasting four daily radio shows out of Great Britain through the British Broadcasting Corporation (BBC). These broadcasts were intended to boost the morale of people back home, and they served as a means to transmit news of the war.

The news was very bad. After German tanks and bombers pummeled Poland on September 1, 1939, Great Britain and

NICHOLAS WINTON

At the end of 1938, a twenty-nine-year-old English stockbroker named Nicholas Winton was on vacation in Prague after thousands of Jews fled there from the Sudetenland, which Germany had annexed in October. The desperate refugees took shelter in makeshift camps, and lived in fear that Hitler was going to invade Czechoslovakia. They believed that they would be the first to suffer. Nicholas Winton, recognizing how volatile their situation was, decided to act quickly. Without any funding from the British government, he created lists of children who seemed most at risk and managed to assemble a group of sympathizers who would help arrange for the children's transportation to Great Britain. The Czech children would be able to enter the nation if a family member or foster parent agreed to meet them at the station and promised to look after them until they turned seventeen.

From December 1938 to September 1939, Winton supervised the evacuation of 700 mostly Jewish children from Nazi-occupied Czechoslovakia on nine trains from Prague to London. The ninth train, which left Prague on September 3, 1939—the day Great Britain declared war on Germany—was never heard from again. There were 250 children on board.

As a toddler, Madeleine—then known as Madlenka—escaped with her family to London during World War II. As an adult, Albright would credit her family's many moves to different countries for her ability to quickly adapt to new situations and get along with all kinds of people. Even as a child, a family friend noted, the intelligent and bold Madlenka "had to be noticed."

France kept a promise they had made and declared war on Germany, marking the beginning of World War II, a bloody and costly global conflict ultimately responsible for the deaths of 45 million people. By early 1940, German forces had conquered Denmark, Norway, Belgium, and the Netherlands.

By June 1940, France had surrendered to both Germany and Italy, and an invasion of England was almost inevitable. The Körbels were about to experience the war firsthand.

Hitler's plan was to weaken the British Royal Air Force (RAF) before attacking the nation by land and sea. The idea was that without protection from above, British warships could not survive. In August, the Luftwaffe (Nazi air force) attacked British defenses, radar stations, and RAF installations. The British forces, and the RAF in particular (aided by radar, used for the first time in battle), fought valiantly and intelligently, and proved themselves superior to the Luftwaffe; by the end of August, the Luftwaffe was defeated. In September 1940, however, Hitler initiated his ruthless Blitz campaign, relentlessly assaulting by air such British cities as London, Manchester, Nottingham, and Coventry. Schools, stores, churches, and houses were bombed. As air raid sirens sounded, people sought safety in underground shelters. The Battle of Britain continued through October 1940, but the combination of British resolve and technical superiority managed to thwart Nazi plans. The battle represented a decisive turning point in the war—it was the first major loss for the Nazis and it saved Britain from an all-out Nazi invasion.

The war years made a tremendous impression on Madlenka. She once commented in an interview:

> I remember the war distinctly. We were in London during the blitz. I remember what it was like to come out of the air-raid shelter and see London bombed. I remember spending huge portions of my life in air-raid shelters singing "A Hundred Green Bottles Hanging on the Wall." I remember . . . they had just invented some kind of steel table. They said if your house was bombed and you were under the table, you would survive. We had this table, and we ate on the table and we slept under the table, and we played around the table.[10]

The Körbels moved a lot during the war. As Hitler stepped up his bombing campaign in spring 1941 (part of his strategy of intimidation), the family stayed in a seaside town on the southern coast of England and then moved into a farmhouse owned by Jan Körbel and his family, located in a town called Berkhamsted. It was in Berkhamsted that the Körbels converted to Roman Catholicism. Josef, Mandula, Madlenka, and Jan were all baptized. Although Albright claims to have no memory of her baptism, she once said, "As a child I was a very serious Catholic. . . . I went to confession all the time."[11]

Meanwhile, children and others of all ages with just as much of a Jewish heritage as Madlenka were being subjected to untold horrors back in Czechoslovakia and all over Europe. For some time, reports of savage acts against Jews and other groups had been leaking out from Central and Eastern Europe. There were rumors that Jews and others deemed "undesirable"—including homosexuals, Christian and Catholic Poles, the physically disabled, and so-called Gypsies—were being rounded up by the Nazis and corralled into internment camps. Scattered reports claimed that people were being starved, tortured, gassed to death, or shot. Many people chose not to believe what they heard. Though the full extent of the devastation the Nazis inflicted on the Jews and other minorities would not be known for some time. Josef Körbel had a hand in the dissemination of some of this information across the airwaves.

Some of Körbel's colleagues found his tendency to conceal his Jewish heritage troubling. Avigdon Dagan, in charge of cultural propaganda for the Czech government in exile, said, "[Körbel] was never ready to admit he was a Jew. . . . Whenever you started to talk about Jewish matters, he clammed up. . . . Or he would start talking about something else. For me, this was difficult to swallow."[12] As word of the mass deportation of Jews and others into concentration camps reached London, Josef Körbel surely must have wondered about the fate of his family and friends. His parents, Olga and Arnost, along with his sister Margareta, her husband, and her daughter Milena, and many other members of his and Mandula's extended families, were still back home, and their fate was in the hands of the Nazis.

THE TIDE TURNS

On June 22, 1941, the course of the war dramatically shifted as Hitler, frustrated by his failures in Britain, invaded Russia, defying a pact he had signed with Russia's leader Stalin less than two years earlier. Now the Nazis were fighting on two fronts. The tide truly started to turn after the Japanese bombed Pearl Harbor, Hawaii, on December 7, 1941.

While the war in Europe was raging on, Japan had taken advantage of the opportunity to expand into China and Southeast Asia. In order to try to stop Japan from gaining too much power, the United States imposed sanctions. After Japanese forces moved into Indochina, President Roosevelt halted trade relations with Japan. While the United States and Japan negotiated to prevent war, Japan launched a surprise attack on the United States at Pearl Harbor. More than 2,000 people were killed. President Franklin Roosevelt called December 7, 1941 a "day that will live in infamy" and declared war on Japan the following day.

In 1942, the U.S. navy decimated Japanese airpower in the Battle of Midway; the Russians repelled Germans armies from Moscow, the Caucusus, and Stalingrad; and the British defeated German and Italian forces on the Mediterranean coast of Africa. By 1943, the Allies were forging full-steam ahead, and they assumed the offensive role on all fronts.

Meanwhile, in October 1942, Mandula had given birth to her second child, Kathy. Madlenka was just beginning to read, and Dagmar, who was then fourteen, helped look after both of her younger cousins. Shortly after this time, Josef and his family moved to a comfortable middle-class suburb called Walton-on-Thames, where they shared a rented house with another Czechoslovak refugee named Eduard Goldstucker and his family. Little Madlenka had lost her Czech accent (by now she even spoke with a bit of a cockney accent) and attended first grade at the Ingomar School. She spent her free time riding her bicycle, playing field hockey, playing cards, and even pretending she was a priest.

Madlenka was also beginning to learn about politics. In later years, she remembered hearing her parents discussing Czechoslovakia's past and what the country was like before World War II:

> Mostly, they spoke of politics, about how the period between the world wars was a golden time for Czechoslovakia. My parents had been in their twenties, and [my father] was a diplomat, and they talked more about being the first generation of adults in free Czechoslovakia. This was their pride and this is what I grew up with.[13]

As an adult, Madeleine Albright retains an especially vivid memory of listening to the radio with her father. She was seven years old, and the radio was broadcasting news that U.S. forces had freed the western part of Czechoslovakia. General Patton's troops had pushed the Nazis out of Pilsen. Albright recalled, "I remember the broadcasts as the Nazis were pushed back across Czechoslovakia, and I remember my parents cheering and wishing they had gone further."[14]

By April 1945, German cities had been devastated by a sweeping Allied bombing campaign, and Hitler, watching as his country collapsed, committed suicide in his Berlin bunker while Russians pummeled the city. By June 1945, the Allies had definitively defeated the Nazis in Europe; two months later, after the United States dropped atomic bombs on Hiroshima and Nagasaki, the Japanese surrendered. World War II, the biggest war in history, was finally over.

Daughter of
a Statesman
1945–1948

"From Stettin in the Baltic to Trieste in the Adriatic, an Iron Curtain
has descended across the Continent . . . The Dark Ages may return
on the gleaming wings of science. Beware, I say. Time may be short."
—Winston Churchill, 1946

As the Allies made their march toward the German capital of
Berlin, the seemingly unbelievable reports of the Nazis' mass
slaughter of Jews and other "undesirables" were confirmed
as forces uncovered undeniable evidence of one gruesome
atrocity after another. In July 1944, Soviet troops liberated
the Maidanek camp in Poland, where they estimated the Nazis
had murdered more than 1.5 million Jews of Eastern-European
descent. In January 1945, the Soviets found hundreds of
corpses of recently executed people and thousands of starving
and disease-ridden prisoners when they liberated the

Auschwitz-Birkenau camps. American and British soldiers found thousands more people barely alive and human bodies piled up in mass graves when they freed the Buchenwald, Dachau, and Belsen camps. It soon came to light that some of these concentration camps provided slave labor (where prisoners were worked and essentially starved to death), but other camps were established solely for the purpose of extermination, usually in gas chambers. (The most notorious of these Nazi death camps was Auschwitz-Birkenau, in Poland, where more than four million people were executed between 1940 and 1945.) The total number of Jews murdered in the

THE AUSCHWITZ-BIRKENAU EXTERMINATION CAMP

In 1940, the Nazis established a concentration camp in the town of Oswiecim, Poland. The town's name was eventually changed to Auschwitz. Over the next few years, the camp was expanded to include Auschwitz I, Auschwitz II-Birkenau, and Auschwitz III-Monowitz, and more than forty smaller camps. Initially the site served as an internment camp for Polish people; later, Romani peoples (also known as Gypsies), Soviet prisoners of war, and others were also held there. In 1942, the camp was converted into the central location of the most massive and monstrous murder campaign in world history. As part of Hitler's "final solution to the Jewish problem"—the plan to systematically destroy Europe's entire Jewish population—Jewish men, women, and children, along with Romanis, homosexuals, the mentally retarded, and others viewed as weak or troublesome, were deported to Auschwitz and sent to their deaths. Most of them were slaughtered in the gas chambers upon immediate arrival at the camp (only about 25 percent of the prisoners who first arrived were deemed fit for work). Some prisoners at the site were subjected to the barbarous medical experiments of Dr. Joseph Mengele. Between 1 million and 2.5 million people died at Auschwitz.

Holocaust (Great Massacre), or Shoah (as it is known in Hebrew), is estimated at more than six million; an additional five million people, including Christian and Catholic Poles and other "undesirable" groups, were also murdered.

Toward the end of the war, some Eastern Europeans living abroad learned about the fate of their relatives who had stayed behind. When Terezin (the miserable ghetto that served as a way station for tens of thousands of Jews on their way to Auschwitz or other camps in the east) was liberated by the Russians in May 1945, the Red Cross released lists of people who had perished there. This is how Madlenka's cousin Dagmar learned that her mother had died of typhoid. She has also said that Josef Körbel found out about the death of his father Arnost (most likely of typhoid, too) in this manner as well.

It wasn't until the Körbels returned to Prague that Josef and Mandula realized the full extent of the carnage the Nazis had wrought on their family. Josef went back first, followed two months later by Mandula, Madlenka, Kathy, and Dagmar. When they arrived, people were wandering around the streets of the city, searching for food and desperately trying to locate relatives. Thousands of survivors met daily in Prague's Customs House to share information about former camp inmates. Dagmar heard from a man named Jiri Barbier that her father had been gassed at Auschwitz. The two men had been on the same transport to the death camp, and they had made a pact that if one were killed, the other would track down his relatives and tell them what had happened.

It would take several years for the Körbels to reconstruct the details of what had happened to their loved ones. Eventually Josef and Mandula learned that their parents (the three who were still alive at the beginning of the war) had been murdered by the Nazis, along with two dozen close relatives. Olga Körbel had been sent to Auschwitz and was executed in the gas chamber. Ruzena Spiegelova was sent to Terezin, then transported to Poland, where she was most likely gassed. Milena, Dagmar's young sister (who was twelve at the time), died at Auschwitz. Other cousins, aunts, uncles, great aunts and uncles, and friends were shot, gassed, or died of starvation or illness. The Czech Jewish community was almost entirely destroyed. More than 70,000 Bohemian and Moravian Jews had been executed in the Holocaust.

According to Dagmar, Madlenka, who was eight years old at the time, was deemed too young to be told the horrific truth about her relatives. She was informed that they had died during the war, but not how. Madeleine Albright does not remember her grandparents in Prague. She has said, "If you're eight years old and you are told that your grandparents died and you think of grandparents as being old people then you don't question it."[1] She also claimed that she had no idea that any of her family members had been killed in the Holocaust until 1997. That year, Michael Dobbs, a reporter for the *Washington Post,* came across the startling information while researching the family history of the United States' first female secretary of state.

This topic generated a fair share of controversy. It seemed impossible to some people that a person of Albright's intellect and savvy would be ignorant of her own family background. Some people questioned Josef and Mandula's judiciousness in withholding the truth from their children. Yet this practice of never mentioning the atrocities that befell them and their families during the Holocaust was common among many European Jews of the time; their focus was on the future.

Upon their return to Czechoslovakia, the Körbels, along with seventeen-year-old Dagmar, moved into a luxurious second-floor apartment in the heart of Prague. Dagmar has said that there was barely any mention of their dead relatives in the strict Körbel household. She said, "I was told

I had to brace myself and do as best I could. My uncle said you must take things as they are."[2]

One of the first things that Josef and Mandula did was officially change their family name. In July of 1945, they dropped the umlaut from Körbel because Korbel without the umlaut altered the name's pronunciation, making it sound and look more Czech and less Jewish. It seemed to represent the final break from their Jewish past.

A POSITION IN BELGRADE

As the war was winding down, Eduard Beneš concentrated much of his energy on strengthening ties with the Communist Soviet Union. After the disappointment of the Munich Pact and what many viewed as the West's betrayal of Czechoslovakia, Beneš believed that allying his country with the Soviet Union would help protect it from German aggression. In December 1943, Beneš had signed an agreement with the Soviets, which stipulated that Czechoslovakia would be reconstructed without Soviet interference. The agreement also provided that Beneš would have to allow room for Czech Communists in the postwar government.

Through the spring of 1945, Josef Korbel was an essential part of a team that was committed to getting the Czech government back on its feet in Prague. In September of that year, when Josef was just thirty-six years old, Beneš appointed him the first Czech ambassador to Yugoslavia. Korbel accepted the three-year assignment. Thus, when Madlenka was eight years old, the Korbels packed their bags and left Czechoslovakia once again. Dagmar stayed behind in Prague with a relative.

Beneš trusted Korbel completely and had faith that he would perform well in his new post, which required an ample dose of diplomatic skill. Yugoslavia, led by Marshal Tito, was now under strict Communist control, and Czechoslavakia was still partially aligned with the West.

Before Korbel left for Belgrade, Beneš said to him, "Keep your eyes open. Personally, I have little confidence in Tito. He is, above all, a Communist who succeeds in concealing his real aims by temporary nationalist propaganda."[3]

Yugoslavia was a ravaged country when the Korbel family arrived. Ten percent of the population had died during World War II, civil wars, and the Communist revolution of 1944, and many towns and villages were destroyed. Anyone who had democratic leanings was considered an enemy of the Communist regime. Tito's government was unforgiving in its elimination of the opposition. Korbel was shunned by several of his friends and colleagues he had become acquainted with during his prewar assignment in the city. Even those who spoke with him behaved strangely in his presence.

The family lived in a spacious and beautiful apartment in the Czech embassy where Madlenka was doted on by servants and nannies. Her father enlisted her help in greeting dignitaries during welcoming ceremonies. At such events, she wore traditional Czech clothing and presented large bouquets of flowers to visitors. Josef and Mandula seemed to have had very high hopes for their eldest daughter, but they were also very strict. She and her siblings (Mandula gave birth to son Jan, later called John, in 1947) were expected to obey their parents, to be prompt, and to complete their homework every day.

Because her parents didn't want Madlenka to be exposed to any sort of Communist influence—they were adamantly against any type of dictatorship—they hired a Czech governess to tutor her at home. Madlenka performed remarkably well academically, yet she had few playmates and spent the bulk of her time with her governess. In the fall of 1947, when she was ten, her parents sent her to the Prealpina School in Chexbres, Switzerland. She had been several steps ahead of other children her age in Belgrade, so her parents

The ten-year-old Madlenka became "Madeleine" at the challenging, French-influenced boarding school her parents sent her to in Switzerland. Typical to her experiences, Madeleine's time in Switzerland would be brief; just a year later she would join her parents, who had fled Communist Czechoslovakia, in London.

thought the boarding school would be better suited to her academic ability.

Boarding school was difficult for Madlenka at first. She initially spoke no French, and she had no friends at the school. Her childhood name of Madlenka was changed to "Madeleine" at this time. She has said of the school, "I hated it at first. And I didn't come home for Christmas that first year. My parents felt I should stay there."[4] Young Madeleine eventually adapted and thrived, just as she had done in London, and just as she would do the rest of her life. She later said, "My mother always taught me to be open and friendly with new people. She said I could learn a lot from them, and she was right."[5] Still, Albright's feelings of not entirely belonging never left her, and throughout her life, she would continue to feel like an outsider while at the same time cultivating an ability to blend in with different types of people and make them feel comfortable.

COMMUNISTS STAGE A COUP

While Josef was doing his duty in Yugoslavia, Tito was swiftly consolidating his power, censoring the press, stripping people of their liberties, and nationalizing factories and other enterprises. Major political changes were also afoot in Czechoslovakia. After the elections of 1946, Beneš continued to serve as president, but the Communist Party garnered more votes than any other party. Consequently, Klement Gottwalk, the leader of the Czech Communists, became prime minister. In the summer of 1947, the United States invited Czechoslovakia to participate in talks about rebuilding Europe under the Marshall Plan. The Czechs accepted, but Soviet leader Josef Stalin instructed Gottwalk to withdraw his support. Through the beginning of 1948, Czech Communist activity accelerated. In February of that year, the Communists staged a *putsch*, or coup. They succeeded in pushing out Democratic ministers, forcing Beneš to agree to establish a new Communist-run government. The Communists now held total control of Tomás Masaryk's formerly democratic country.

Shortly after the coup, on March 10, 1948, Josef's friend Jan Masaryk was found dead in the courtyard of the Foreign Ministry of Prague. It was unclear whether he jumped, fell, or was pushed out of the window. Josef was grief-stricken, devastated. A friend said that Josef "regarded Masaryk as the last hope for democracy."[6] Josef came to believe that Masaryk had been murdered by Soviet agents. Both he and Mandula flew to Prague for the funeral. They also met with Dagmar. It would be the last time Dagmar would ever see them. It was a tense and frightening time, and the Korbels felt forced, once again, to flee their beloved home country—this time for good.

Josef had been offered a position representing Czechoslovakia in a United Nations committee formed to try to resolve a dispute between India and Pakistan over the Kashmir region. He had been working abroad on the Indian subcontinent around the time the Czech government was overthrown. This position created the opportunity for the family to escape the Czech Communist government and the Iron Curtain that then separated East from West.

In the summer of 1948, Josef told Mandula and the children to leave Yugoslavia for London. Mandula boarded the train in Belgrade with Kathy and John, then made a stop in Switzerland to visit Madeleine. When they arrived in London, the family settled into a small flat in a place called Earl's Court. When Madeleine's school term was over, she flew to London to join them and was promptly enrolled in the Lycée Français. Albright later called it "the hardest single school I went to in my life."[7]

Meanwhile, Josef was involved in the Kashmir situation and also trying to track down visas to enter the United States. His UN connections enabled him to get visas for his family and even for their eighteen-year-old Yugoslav maid, Fanci Mencinger. On November 5, 1948, Mandula, Madeleine, Kathy, John, and Fanci all boarded the SS *America* in Southhampton. Carrying twenty-one pieces of luggage and traveling first class, they were bound for New York City.

Later that month, Josef had a discussion with Vladimir Clementis, the Communist foreign minister with whom he had worked closely and who was even somewhat of a friend. Clementis asked Korbel his opinion of the new Czech government. Korbel replied:

> Mr. Minister . . . you know I am not a Communist, and therefore I cannot be but critical towards the events at home. . . . I shall tell you frankly that Communism and the Communist regime are unacceptable to me. . . . I cannot fight for Communism.[8]

A month after that, Josef was formally dismissed from the Czechoslovak Foreign Ministry. Josef Korbel was now considered an enemy of the state. On December 17, 1948, he boarded the HMS *Queen Mary* and headed toward New York to join his wife and children.

5

American Girl

1948–1959

"By attending Wellesley, these women have been 'given the ideal preparation to serve at the very heart of the home.'"

—Secretary of Defense Neil McElroy,
Wellesley College commencement speech, 1959

Madeleine's voyage on the SS *America* was rocky and difficult. Fanci and Mandula were seasick for the bulk of the six-day trip—the two stayed in their cabins while Madeleine tended to Kathy and John. On November 11, 1948, they all stood on deck as the boat entered New York Harbor. The sight of the Statue of Liberty, a potent symbol of American liberty and opportunity, must have filled eleven-year-old Madeleine and the entire Korbel family with an enormous sense of relief and hope. After years of fleeing oppression and persecution, they would never again have to live in fear;

they would never again worry about losing their rights. They were finally going to achieve the freedom that had eluded them. The United States granted Josef Korbel and his family political asylum, and the Korbels were on their way to becoming American citizens (Albright officially became a U.S. citizen in 1957).

It is difficult to describe just how much young Madeleine's experiences, and those of her father and mother, influenced the future UN ambassador and secretary of state. One friend of Albright explained:

> Picture your life. Your job, your friends, your house, the school that your children attend, and the playground on which they play. One day it's there and everything is wonderful. And the next day, tanks from a German Special Army Panzer Division are rolling down the streets and Nazi storm troopers begin to round up your friends, your coworkers, your family. In a matter of days, everything you own and care about is taken from you. And on top of that, a battalion of the best-trained soldiers in the world are hunting you down, trying to kill you. As amazing as it sounds, that was Madeleine Albright's life as a little girl.[1]

It is equally as difficult to describe just how much the premise of freedom and democracy meant, and mean, to Madeleine Albright. As President Bill Clinton once articulated, "She watched her world fall apart, and ever since, she has dedicated her life to spreading to the rest of the world the freedom and tolerance her family found here in America."[2]

Albright has pointed to one event as "the beginning of [her] political consciousness."[3] Right before they boarded the SS *America* in Southhampton, Madeleine and her family listened to the 1948 U.S. presidential election results on the radio. They were exuberant when they heard that Democrat

Harry S Truman had secured a last-minute upset against New York Republican governor Thomas E. Dewey. Although public opinion had heavily favored Dewey, the incumbent President Truman (who as vice president assumed the presidency when Franklin D. Roosevelt died in April 1945) narrowly and surprisingly defeated Dewey. There was no question that Madeleine, like her parents, was a Democrat. The progressivism and reform-minded precepts of the Democratic Party appealed greatly to the Korbels' sense of justice and equality. Madeleine Albright has remained an outspoken advocate of Democratic principles throughout her political life.

A NEW LIFE

While Josef continued to concentrate on the Kashmir issue with the UN until the end of 1948, Madeleine attended a public grade school in Long Island. By this time, she was used to changes in her environment, but she still often felt like an outsider—she not only dressed differently from her schoolmates but she was also forbidden by her more old-fashioned parents to attend boy-girl parties. One day she realized that her voice sounded different from that of her classmates. It was then that she was alerted to the fact that she had a British accent. Because she so wanted to fit in, she practiced speaking with an American accent. Eventually she sounded just like a typical American.

After Josef found a job as a professor of international relations at the University of Denver in 1949, the family got into their green Ford and drove across the country to their new home in Colorado. They moved into a small apartment in downtown Denver, in housing provided by the university.

It was there that Josef Korbel embarked on an impressive career in academia. He soon got a permanent appointment at the University of Denver, and in 1959, was appointed dean of the Graduate School for International Studies. During his years in the United States, he also served as visiting professor at such illustrious institutions as Harvard, Columbia, MIT, and Oxford. Korbel wrote several well-regarded books, including *Tito's Communism* (1951), *The Communist Subversion of Czechoslovakia* (1965), and *Twentieth-Century Czechoslovakia* (1976). In the latter book, Korbel criticized the Nazi dismemberment of his native country, but, curiously, never mentioned the Holocaust. He became somewhat famous for staunchly defending U.S. involvement in Vietnam at a time when it was widely reviled among academics and students. Korbel felt that it was necessary to intervene to prevent the expansion of Communism.

In spite of his views on the Vietnam War, Korbel was very popular with his students. Many of them visited the Korbel home. Young Madeleine listened closely to their conversations and often participated in the lively household discussions about politics and foreign policy. Albright later recalled, "In my parents' home, we talked about international relations all the time, the way some families talk about sports or other things around the dinner table."[4]

MADELEINE'S TEEN YEARS

Madeleine was developing a passion for international policy, and at the same time shaping the strong beliefs that would influence her career in politics. She acknowledges that her father's influence was vital: "A great deal of what I did, I did because I wanted to be like my father."[5] "My own worldview consists largely of ideas my father implanted on me," she has said. "He was a great intellectual humanist."[6]

Indeed, Madeleine had tremendous admiration for her father, and the two shared a special relationship, in large part because she was so engaged in subjects that interested him. While Josef was writing books about Eastern Europe, Madeleine drafted essays on similar topics in school.

In many ways, Josef Korbel was an old-fashioned disciplinarian. Madeleine's brother has said, "He was a strict,

European parent. . . . It never dawned on us not to respect our parents, and we were punished when we did something wrong. The most severe form of punishment was when our father wouldn't talk to us for a week."[7]

The children were often under a lot of pressure. Though Kathy and John rebelled against Josef and his strict ways occasionally, Madeleine usually obeyed and pleased him. Kathy later said, "Madeleine was the responsible one."[8]

Madeleine Albright has mentioned only two serious arguments with her father. The first occurred shortly before she enrolled in high school. Her father insisted that she attend the exclusive, private Kent School for Girls, which had offered her a scholarship. Madeleine wanted to study at the large local public high school because she craved a typical American teen experience. She ultimately succumbed to her father's wishes and later admitted that the private school was the right choice.

The other argument concerned Madeleine's high school prom. Josef wouldn't allow Madeleine and her date to ride alone in her date's car. After an extended discussion, Josef finally permitted them to ride together, but only under the condition that he follow them in his own car. "To this day, I will never forget the mortification," she said years later. "I didn't see that boy again."[9]

In many ways, Madeleine was a quintessential American teenager. Eager to blend in, she started wearing clothes that other teenagers of the 1950s wore—like just the right camel-hair coat and crewneck sweaters. She once said of that time, "I spent a lot of time worrying, trying to make sure that I would fit in. . . . I wanted very much to be an American."[10] Madeleine skied, played field hockey, and swam. She learned to play the piano and sang with the Glee Club. She also continued to practice Roman Catholicism.

In other ways, she was highly atypical. As a teenager, she knew substantially more about international relations than most adults did. Albright has said, "I think I was pretty boring in high school. I was a foreign policy wonk even then."[11] Self-disciplined and serious, she even set up an international relations club at school, and made herself president. While a student, she won a contest sponsored by the United Nations.

One of her classmates, Stephanie Allen, said that Madeleine seemed more motivated than the rest of the students and singled out Madeleine's ability to get along with people:

> She studied hard. It was a class of very bright girls. Madeleine was not the brightest girl in the class, but she was the most well-rounded person. She was a good friend. She could laugh and play with the rest of us. She did her studies, but she didn't rub it in.[12]

She was also known for drive, intensity, and independent thinking, as the caption beneath her yearbook photo attests: "You will often find [Madeleine] taking a definite stand on matters, staunchly saying, 'You guys, this just proves it!'"[13]

WELLESLEY

In 1955, Madeleine Korbel was one of sixteen graduates of the Kent School for Girls. Although she got into all five colleges she applied to (Stanford University, the University of Pennsylvania, Mount Holyoke, the University of Denver, and Wellesley College), she accepted a scholarship to attend the prestigious Wellesley College in Wellesley, Massachusetts. At the time, she was interested primarily in two fields of study—politics and journalism, just like her father when he was a young man.

In college, Madeleine stood out for her dedication and diligence. She was also exceptionally detailed and methodical—she even organized her meticulous notes into a color-coded binder. At a time when most women were taught to become proper young ladies and good mothers and housewives, Madeleine was dramatically different. "She was very driven in a way that was not standard for women of the fifties," one friend said.[14] Another classmate said, "Madeleine was definitely one of the people who were more goal-oriented than the rest of us. That she should have accomplished so much is not terribly surprising. Everything was there at Wellesley: her intelligence, her drive, her thoroughness."[15]

Madeleine loved Wellesley. She indulged her interest in politics by campaigning for Democratic presidential candidate Adlai Stevenson when he faced Dwight Eisenhower in the 1956 election. Although most of her fellow students were Republican, Madeleine was a proud Democrat. She would take trips to Boston to collect money for the Democrats, and she found participating in the grassroots campaign to be a wholly positive and invigorating experience. She also wrote articles about campus issues (her first piece was titled "Hamburgers and Harvard, Diets and Dates") and politics for her school newspaper, eventually becoming associate news editor.

Madeleine's interest in journalism led to her working as an intern for her hometown newspaper, the *Denver Post*, in the summer of 1957. While there, she wrote stories about weddings and worked in the company's file room. It was at the newspaper that she met Joseph Medill Patterson Albright, another summer intern who was a student at Williams College, in Williamstown, Massachusetts. Albright was from one of the most successful and well-known families in journalism, and he was the heir to an impressive newspaper fortune. His father was the founder of the New York *Daily News*; his aunt, Alicia Patterson Guggenheim, was the founder and owner of the Long Island, New York-based *Newsday*.

Joseph Albright was a private, quiet, and studious young man. He and Madeleine shared an interest in politics and journalism, and the two started to date. Josef and Mandula Korbel approved of Joe, and they grew to love him. Initially, Madeleine had no idea that Joe came from such a prominent, high-society background, and indeed she was at first overwhelmed by the imposing wealth of the Albright-Guggenheim clan. Nevertheless, their relationship quickly grew serious. When Madeleine returned to the Wellesley campus her junior year, she surprised her friends with the news that she had been "pinned"—Joe had given her his fraternity pin, symbolizing their pre-engagement. Their true engagement was announced on December 29, 1959, in a three-paragraph story in the *New York Times*.

Through her last year at Wellesley, Madeleine devoted much of her time to the research and writing of her senior thesis. Her topic was the Communist subversion of Czechoslovak democracy, a subject of supreme interest not only to her father but to Madeleine as well. She also spent much of her year planning for her marriage to Joe. Madeleine's college years were

THE FEMINIST MOVEMENT

The women's movement in the United States dates back to 1848, when such courageous women as Elizabeth Cady Stanton, Lucretia Coffin Mott, and Susan B. Anthony fought hard for the right to vote. Women gained suffrage in 1920, but they still faced significant social and legal barriers to educational and economic opportunities. In the 1960s and 1970s, a "second wave" of feminism challenged traditional stereotypes of women, especially the perception that they define themselves through their husbands and their children. Feminists of the era were also concerned with such issues as equality in political representation, matters of sexuality, changing family roles, and discrimination in the workplace. Groups such as NOW (the National Organization for Women, formed in 1966) pushed for legislation regarding equal pay, childcare, property rights, and abortion rights. One result of the movement was that in 1997, 59.8 percent of women older than sixteen were working; in 1960, only 37.7 percent of women in that age group had jobs. Two important feminist books of this era were Simone de Beauvoir's *The Second Sex* (1949) and Betty Friedan's *The Feminine Mystique* (1963).

a strange time for women. The feminist movement had not really gained steam yet—Betty Friedan, author of the seminal *The Feminine Mystique,* conducted the bulk of her research in 1959. There was an enormous amount of social pressure at Wellesley for students to focus on marrying and raising children, despite the high quality of their education.

In 1959, Madeleine Korbel graduated with honors from Wellesley, earning a bachelor's degree in political science. The commencement speaker at the college that year was the U.S. secretary of defense, Neil McElroy. During his speech, he emphasized that the women of Wellesley should concentrate most on raising the next generation of educated citizens. Little did he know that in the audience that day was a Wellesley graduate who would one day not only raise three well-educated citizens but would also become the nation's first female secretary of state—the highest office in the land ever to be held by a woman.

Domestics and
Doctoral Studies

1959–1968

"After two world wars, the Holocaust, multiple genocides and count-
less conflicts, we must ask how long it will be before we are able
to rise above the national, racial and gender distinctions that
divide us, and embrace the common humanity that binds us."
—Madeleine Albright

Three days after her graduation, Madeleine and Joe Albright
were married in an Episcopalian service. (Although Madeleine
had been devoted to the Roman Catholic Church, she
converted to her husband's family's Episcopalian faith.) Joe
Albright was an army reservist, and upon their return from
their honeymoon in the Caribbean, he was sent to military
training at the army base in Fort Leonard Wood, Missouri.
Madeleine soon joined him in Missouri, where she worked for
a very short stint at the *Rolla Daily News*, earning $35 a week.

When Joe completed his army training, the couple moved to Chicago, and Joe started a job at the *Sun Times*, owned by a friend of the Albright family. Madeline wanted to work there, too, but, over dinner one night, an editor told her that she could not be employed by the same paper as her husband, and it would not be right if she worked at a competing paper in the city. "You have an obligation to your husband to find another line of work," others in the industry said to her.[1] This attitude made her angry, but she later said that she "wasn't mad enough to fight."[2] She later said, "As it turns out, I was very lucky, because I would have been a lousy reporter. . . . I understood. I went and got a different job. It's very different today."[3]

She soon found employment as a researcher for *Encyclopœdia Britannica*. Then, in 1961, Joe was named the city editor of *Newsday*. His Aunt Alicia, who treated Joe like a son, had been very impressed by a front-page story twenty-three-year-old Joe had written about presidential nominee Richard Nixon. Joe had hidden in a hotel bathroom during the Republican National Convention to get the scoop. His aunt asked him to work for her, and although Joe's mother was opposed to her son's immediate immersion into the stress and frenzy of the high-power newspaper world, Joe insisted he was ready for it. In April of that year, the Albrights moved to Garden City, Long Island, and Joseph Albright began working for his aunt.

MOTHERHOOD AND GRADUATE SCHOOL

The following June, Albright gave birth to twin daughters. Named Anne and Alice, the girls were born six weeks premature. Because they weighed just a little over three pounds each, they had to be kept in incubators, and Albright was not even allowed to touch them because they were highly vulnerable to infection. As a way of distracting herself from worrying about her babies, Albright enrolled in an intensive eight-week Russian language course at Columbia University.

Two months after their birth, her daughters were finally

Albright gave birth to her twin daughters, Anne and Alice, in 1961. Although Albright loved being a mother, she found the typical homemaker's role too limiting for her active mind and many interests. She later recalled watching soap operas during the day while her husband worked and thinking, "I didn't go to college to do this."

healthy and able to leave hospital. Although Madeleine and Joe had an active social life that included regularly visiting Alicia and Harry Guggenheim's posh estate, Albright's life at this time revolved primarily around caring for the twins. This routine proved unsatisfying to Albright; she didn't feel challenged. "I went nuts that year," she has said.[4] "I kind of sat there during the day, feeding them, watching soap operas, and I thought, 'I didn't go to college to do this.'"[5] She decided to go back to school to become a professor.

MIDDLE SCHOOL
LIBRARY

In 1962, however, Joe was transferred to *Newsday's* Washington, D.C., bureau for a long-term assignment—covering the State Department. The Albrights rented a house in the center of stylish Georgetown, and Joe continued to impress his colleagues and superiors with his aggressive reporting and his excellent ability to dig up stories. Madeleine and Joe loved Washington and the company of their lively circle of friends. It was an exciting time to be in the capital city. The young and charismatic president John F. Kennedy had brought a sense of renewal and hope to Democrats like Madeleine and Joe. At the time, tension between the United States and Soviet Union was mounting, so there was much talk about issues that Madeleine Albright cared passionately about, particularly America's role in preventing the spread of Communism.

Albright began studying for her doctorate in political science with an emphasis on international relations at the Johns Hopkins University's School of Advanced International Affairs. Although she hired housekeepers to help take care of her children, she was an incredibly busy woman, stretched in many different directions. She was becoming remarkably adept at managing her time. It was a rather unusual lifestyle for a woman of Albright's era, but she was simply doing what she felt she had to do. She has commented about that time, "I think I was basically listening to some inner need. I wanted to do something interesting and useful with my life."[6] In 1963, Joe's Aunt Alicia died while undergoing surgery for a stomach ulcer. Harry Guggenheim immediately named Joe assistant to the publisher, and the Albrights were sent back to Long Island.

The Albright family headed back to New York and moved into a lovely nineteenth-century clapboard house in a wealthy area of Oyster Bay on Long Island. They were able to afford the home because Alicia Guggenheim had bequeathed a large part of her estate to Joe. In September 1963, Madeleine Albright enrolled in Columbia University's Graduate School of Arts and Sciences to continue pursuing her doctorate in political science. Two or three times a week, she drove to the Columbia campus, and she spent a lot of time poring over books and taking her typically meticulous notes. While she studied hard, she somehow managed to maintain an active social life that included hosting dinner parties and playing tennis. The Albrights were now rich, and they had many high-society and powerful connections, yet in many ways they still appeared to be an unassuming couple whose lives revolved around her studies at Columbia, his work, and the kids. The housekeepers certainly helped her enormously, yet Albright still found the time to cook, shop for food, and drive the children to their activities. Albright's daughter Anne has commented:

> My sisters and I never felt that our mother didn't have enough time for us. She's always done the ordinary things that mothers do: getting us up in the mornings and ready for school, helping us with our homework. We used to do our homework together. . . . On Fridays she would do the grocery shopping while my sisters and I were horseback riding or taking ballet classes or guitar lessons. She was just the coolest mom. We had a wonderful family life.[7]

Due to all the demands of motherhood and her marriage to a man whose job forced the family to move almost constantly, it would take Albright thirteen years to complete her doctorate.

PRAGUE AND COLUMBIA

In 1967, the Albrights had another daughter, Katherine, their last child. That same year, Joe and Madeleine Albright decided to travel to Eastern Europe with some friends while their children remained home with their nanny. They toured Vienna, Budapest, and Belgrade, and then Albright visited as many relatives and friends in Prague as she could, including her cousin Dagmar. The entire trip to Communist Czechoslovakia was tense and difficult. They worried that the secret police would follow them. At the time, Jewish people were being harassed; many Czechs were warning visitors to stay away from the country.

One of the people Albright went to see was her mother's cousin Petr Novak, the sole surviving member of his family— the rest of them had been killed in the Holocaust. During the visit, Albright found out that her father had been on the Gestapo's "most wanted" list and had been sentenced to death in absentia. This revelation very much upset her. Petr, who had been a prodigy at the cello as a teen, also told her his story. While he was at Auschwitz (he was one of the "lucky" prisoners, selected for hard labor), camp guards had cut his wrists so he would never play the cello again. Albright returned to her hotel inconsolable. She fell apart, sobbing, saying, "There but for the grace of God, there but for the grace of God."[8] She kept repeating that Petr had nothing because his family had saved her family. Albright later said that she did not realize Petr Novak was a relative of hers at the time of the visit. Her parents had told her only that his family had hidden Josef and Mandula right after the Nazis invaded Czechoslovakia in 1938.

After the trip, Albright continued to work hard toward her degree at Columbia. Around that time—the late 1960s—while she was diligently working on papers and taking care of her children, there was a widespread and well-organized movement on college campuses across the nation protesting U.S. participation in the war in Vietnam. Communist guerillas of the Vietcong, supported by North Vietnam and backed by the Soviet Union and Communist China, were fighting against the U.S.-backed South Vietnam. Many Americans were infuriated when they saw the newspaper and television reports that graphically revealed the carnage that was being inflicted on the Vietnamese civilian population and the soldiers. Throughout the country, angry students agitated against the United States' massive military buildup in the region (there were more than 500,000 U.S. troops in Vietnam by 1968), and spoke out against what they viewed as American imperialism. Many of the young men who were drafted burned their draft cards in protest. The war was rapidly losing support across the country.

In the early months of 1968, some of the student rebels took over the Columbia campus, barricading buildings with furniture and hanging the Communist flag. Madeleine Albright did not share the students' sense of disillusionment with the United States. Her experiences, and those of her family, made her decidedly pro-United States and anti-Communist. She found the demonstrations annoying and distracting:

> I found [them] a pain in the neck. I don't know how else to describe it. The libraries would be closed. It was such a struggle for me to come in and leave the children. People were doing their oral exams while demonstrators were climbing in the windows. I was in a different period of my life. [9]

ZBIGNIEW BRZEZINSKI

Born in 1928, in Warsaw, Poland, Brzezinski was the son of a Polish diplomat. After a youth spent in France and Germany, he moved to Canada, where he received his bachelor's and master's degrees in political science from McGill University. In 1953, he was awarded his doctorate in political science from Harvard, where he taught before heading up the Institute on Communist Affairs at Columbia University in 1961. During the 1960s, he served as an advisor in both the Kennedy and Johnson administrations. He became well known for his assertiveness and was unwaveringly anti-Communist and anti-Soviet. In 1976, President Jimmy Carter appointed Brzezinski his national security advisor. One of his greatest successes was helping normalize U.S.-Chinese relations, but many of his policies were controversial. He insisted, for example, on backing CIA-run terrorist training camps in Afghanistan, where Islamic fundamentalism flourished.

As a student at Columbia, Albright would develop a strong working relationship with her professor Zbigniew Brzezinski, who was, like her, the child of an Eastern European diplomat. When Brzezinski became national security advisor, he would employ Albright as a congressional liaison, thrusting Albright into the center of national politics. The two, photographed here in 1997, remained friends throughout their careers.

One of Albright's academic advisers at Columbia was Zbigniew Brzezinski, a Polish immigrant who was the director of Columbia's Institute on Communist Affairs. He was one of the few members of the faculty to oppose the student protesters. Albright gravitated to Brzezinski not only because of their common Eastern European background (his father was also a diplomat) but also because they shared stridently anti-Communist views. Professor Brzezinski had a reputation for being demanding and tough and for rarely awarding As. Brzezinski grew very fond of Albright. She performed very well in his classes and the professor admired her tact, organizational abilities, and singular ability to truly get along with others. Albright later wrote, "Brzezinski was the single best professor I ever had. . . . He had great respect for his students. He really drew you out."[10] Their strong professional relationship would open doors for Albright in the future.

In the spring of 1968, Albright was awarded a master's degree in political science (along with a certificate in Russian studies), but there was a wrench thrown into her doctorate plans when her husband accepted a job as associate bureau chief in *Newsday*'s Washington, D.C., Bureau. For the third time in eight years, Albright's life and work were uprooted because of her husband's work. In spite of the disruption, she was intent on achieving her goal, so she and her faculty advisor and her other professors agreed on an arrangement: Albright would work on her doctorate with them long-distance. She would study and conduct research in Washington, then travel to New York when possible.

Climbing
Capitol Hill
1968–1982

"We must be the authors of the history of our age."

—Madeleine Albright

For her dissertation topic, Albright chose to examine the role of the press in Czechoslovakia during a period known as the Prague Spring of 1968. Alexander Dubĉek, who was then head of the Czech Communist Party, had instituted a series of reforms—such as freedom of the press—as part of a movement that was dubbed "Communism with a human face." The Soviet government feared that these liberal actions would weaken the Communist Party and decided to put a stop to them quickly and efficiently. In August 1968, just a few months after the reforms were initiated, Communist troops from the Soviet Union, East Germany, Poland, and Hungary, invaded Czechoslovakia to reimpose totalitarian rule.

Dubĉek was swiftly removed from power, and the reforms were overturned.

This topic allowed Albright to merge her interest in politics and journalism. It also provided her with an opportunity to put her mastery of the Czech language to good use. Albright visited the Library of Congress regularly to sift through and study old newspapers from Prague. She also interviewed, and eventually befriended, many Czech dissidents. One of these dissidents was Jiri Dienstbier, a young radio correspondent and ex-Communist based in New York. Albright and Dienstbier discussed Communism and Czechoslovakia at length, and they discovered that they held some similar views. As Dienstbier recalled, "I was her unofficial consultant." [1]

Dienstbier returned to Czechoslovakia in September 1969. Because he was considered an enemy of the people, the Communists confiscated his passport when he returned to his home country. It was not returned to him until Václav Havel's Velvet Revolution ended forty-one years of Communist rule. When Havel became president of the Czech Republic in 1989, he named Dienstbier his foreign minister. Albright and Dienstbier kept in touch over the years, and it was Dienstbier who introduced Madeleine Albright to Havel when she visited the Czech Republic in 1990.

Albright has said that preparing her dissertation was the most difficult thing she has ever done. Every morning, she would get up at 4:30. She spent many long hours researching and interviewing people and writing. At the same time, she was taking care of her children, entertaining some of Washington's best and brightest stars in politics and media at the Albrights' three-story house near Georgetown University, and serving on the board of Beauvoir Elementary, an elite private school where her twins were enrolled.

RAISING FUNDS AND RAISING CHILDREN

When Anne and Alice were in the second grade at Beauvoir Elementary, Albright, like many other mothers with children at the school, helped out as a volunteer. Her charm, persuasiveness, and drive quickly got her noticed. Though she knew nothing about fundraising, she was put in charge of the school's annual "giving drive." As she later explained, "I got the reputation of getting the job done."[2]

A volunteer from the school, impressed with Albright's work, soon introduced her to Edmund Muskie, a Democratic senator from Maine. Albright admired Muskie, and she agreed to act as a coordinator for an important fundraising dinner for him. Muskie was campaigning for the 1972 presidential election, and the April dinner was viewed as a critical part of the campaign. Albright successfully recruited friends and acquaintances to sell tickets to the dinner, tracked down potential guests, and oversaw even the smallest details for the big event. She wore many different hats in her capacity as coordinator, and although Muskie ended up dropping out of the race, it was a wonderful experience for Albright. She made great contacts, new friends, and kept in touch with Muskie and his wife, Jane. While working with Muskie, Albright developed a reputation for loyalty, hard work, and remarkable organizational abilities.

In the fall of 1972, Albright was elected chair of the board of the Beauvoir School, where she succeeded, among other things, in diversifying the student body. Meanwhile, she was still writing her dissertation and raising her three daughters. Madeleine Albright was a very busy woman, but her daughters say that they did not feel at all neglected. "As kids," wrote one, "we never felt we were being sacrificed for her career. Quite the opposite."[3] Albright was actively involved in their lives, which were filled with sports, music, cultural activities, and lots of friends. She helped them with their homework, got them up in the morning, baked with them, and took them to their classes. In some ways, the Albright household was similar to the Korbel household— full of discussions about international affairs and politics.

Albright was a strong, positive role model for the girls. As her daughter Anne said:

> She always taught us that being charming and attractive is not inconsistent with being smart and aggressive. . . . Each of us sort of assumed we'd go to graduate school; we ended up as two lawyers and a banker. The one thing she really wanted to teach us was—do your best at your job, no matter what it is. She'd said many times that there's no such thing as luck. What you get you work for.[4]

ALBRIGHT ACHIEVES

In 1975, when Edmund Muskie was seeking someone to head up the national fundraising campaign for his reelection to the Senate, Madeleine Albright immediately came to mind. She had a proven track record with fundraising, she was hardworking, and she was especially well connected. Albright accepted Muskie's offer. Although it was a part-time position, it was the first time Albright would be getting paid for her work since the *Encyclopædia Britannica* job.

In 1976, Madeleine Albright achieved another important success: At the age of 39, after years of hard work, she was finally awarded her doctorate. "That made it possible for Senator Muskie to introduce me as Dr. Albright, instead of Madeleine Albright, little housewife," she later wrote.[5] Albright excelled at her job, and she continued to impress Muskie, who made her his chief legislative assistant in August 1976. At the time, there were no female senators, and only a few women held senior staff positions in the Senate. Madeleine Albright was indeed a rarity.

In her new position, Albright coordinated with Senate committee staffs and supervised actions on the Senate floor. She handled various domestic issues, such as health, welfare,

Albright earned Senator Edmund Muskie's respect after she coordinated a fundraising dinner for him. She continued to impress the
senator after she ran his national fundraising campaign in 1975 and
became his chief legislative assistant in 1976. Though the senator
was so difficult to work with that even some of his aides feared
him, Albright was able to handle his volatile nature. When she later
became secretary of state, she hung a picture of the senator outside
her office and acknowledged him as her political "role model."

aging, and Social Security. Muskie had held a seat on the
Senate Foreign Relations Committee since 1971, so she was
able to apply her passion for international relations to her job.
She became well versed on such matters as the Panama Canal
treaties and Middle Eastern affairs.

During her time with Muskie, Albright fine-tuned her
already considerable skills of diplomacy and dealing with all
types of people and personalities. Muskie had a reputation

for being difficult to get along with—many of his aides feared even being in the same room with him. Albright handled his volatile personality well and managed to maintain her composure. Muskie's chief of staff, Leon Billings, commented:

> That she could put with [Muskie's] temper actually served to make Muskie perceive Albright as more of a peer than a staffer. . . . In an office that was always scrambling as the senator seemed to live crisis to crisis, Albright never, ever lost her sense of humor.[6]

In a world populated almost entirely by men, Albright adapted and held her own. "Madeleine never had any trouble being one of the boys," said Billings. "It was clearly a man's world. And the women who were effective in that world participated rather than protested."[7] Albright won the admiration of her peers simply by working hard and by getting the job done. "When she said she was going to get something done, she got it done," a colleague said about her.[8]

Albright worked for Muskie for two years. Later, when she became secretary of state, she hung a portrait of him right outside her office. When she spoke at his funeral years later, she referred to him as her political "role model."

In July 1977, while Albright was enjoying the beginning of an illustrious career in Washington, her beloved father, Josef Korbel, died of pancreatic cancer at the age of sixty-seven. The man who had been her first mentor and role model was unable to witness her early successes, and this pained her deeply. "I was devastated," Albright wrote. "I still am devastated. Every day I wish my father was alive to see what is going on."[9]

THE CARTER ADMINISTRATION

When Democrat James Earl Carter, a peanut farmer from Georgia, narrowly defeated Republican Gerald Ford in the 1976 presidential election in November, he appointed Zbigniew

Brzezinski as his national security advisor. Brzezinski, Albright's professor at Columbia, was also the head of the National Security Council (NSC), which advises the president on foreign policy issues and domestic concerns that might affect national security. After a year on Capitol Hill, he realized that he had to improve his relationships with congressmen. He needed someone with a strong background in congressional operations and relations, someone who knew how to negotiate and who understood how legislation worked on the Hill. Again, Madeleine Albright was a perfect choice. In March 1978, she was appointed by the Carter administration to serve as head congressional liaison for the National Security Council.

The move placed Madeleine Albright in the center of the national political arena. The opportunity brought her more responsibility, a higher salary, and more prestige. In her new post, Albright used her uncanny grasp of "social intelligence" to gain the trust of her colleagues. Her negotiating skills were put to the test regularly, and she handled potentially explosive matters with aplomb. Carter had filled some positions in the White House with colleagues from Georgia, and they worked alongside Washington and New York intellectuals like Brzezinski. Unfortunately, this created tension—Brzezinski was seen as an intellectual snob, and he viewed many Georgians as somewhat ignorant of foreign policy issues. When Albright arrived, she used her savvy and tact to prevent conflict. As writer Michael Dobbs said, "She was one of the very few people on the NSC staff who could go up to Capitol Hill and talk to senators and congressmen in a language they could understand without being obnoxious."[10] She did her utmost to ensure that Brzezinski maintained positive relationships with senators and congressmen. She even encouraged him to engage with them more socially, and thus Brzezinski began attending dinner parties at her Georgetown home. He later credited Albright with "[keeping him] from getting in trouble with Congress."[11]

Albright also gracefully navigated her way through another

difficult situation: managing the tense relationship between Brzezinski and her old boss, Ed Muskie, who was now secretary of state. The two clashed often on matters of foreign policy. Brzezinski was hawkish—inclined to support American military intervention to ward off any threat to American security—and Muskie was more liberal and believed that force was not always necessary. Although it would have been easy to get entangled in their animosity for one another, Albright remained on good terms with both of them, and she miraculously kept communications open between the State Department and the NSC.

Albright plunged headfirst into the issues. Before making a presentation to Congress on the administration's stance on SALT II (the second phase of the Strategic Arms Limitations Talks), she took a biweekly tutorial given by the council's arms-control expert. She started to make her views heard on such issues as normalizing relations with China, the Camp David Accords, and finally, the hostage crisis in Iran. She solidified her reputation as a well-prepared and highly effective, yet unassuming, colleague. One staff member noted, "She was always at the center of things."[12]

It was around this time that Albright says she truly learned to speak out for herself. She recalled that up until then, "I would be in a White House meeting, and I would think of something and not say it because I wasn't sure that it would add to the discussion. Then some man would say what I had been thinking, and it would be hailed as a great idea."[13]

In 1981, after Jimmy Carter battled a struggling economy and unsuccessfully tried to solve the hostage crisis in Iran, he lost the presidential election to Republican Ronald Reagan. Although she had gained some outstanding foreign policy credentials over the last four years, Albright was now out of a job.

A MARRIAGE ENDS

Right after the election, Albright worked with Brzezinski for a short while. He was writing his memoirs, and her task was to note any sections that were considered too sensitive to be published. While working on this project, she was awarded a fellowship from the center for Strategic and International Studies, a think tank in Washington, and she began studying Eastern European and Soviet affairs. She also won a fellowship at the Woodrow Wilson International Center for Scholars at the Smithsonian Institution. As part of that program, she wrote a paper that explored many of the same issues she had examined in her dissertation at Columbia. The paper was

THE SALT TALKS

During the post-World War II years, world politics shifted dramatically as the Soviet Union and the United States emerged as the two new "superpowers." Until 1990, the two nations were engaged in a cold war, an ideological and economic rivalry marked most significantly by the rapid stockpiling of powerful weapons and the threat of nuclear war. In 1969, the two countries started negotiating to curtail the manufacture and use of strategic nuclear missiles. While the discussions were initiated by U.S. President Lyndon Johnson and Soviet President Leonid Brezhnev, SALT I was signed by President Nixon and President Brezhnev in 1972. Under the agreement, both countries agreed to limit their antiballistic missile systems and freeze the number of intercontinental ballistic missiles (ICBMs) and submarine-launched ballistic missiles. In 1973, Brezhnev met with President Gerald Ford to discuss the second phase of the agreement. SALT II was signed by President Carter and President Brezhnev on June 18, 1979. The document banned new ICBMs and limited other strategic launchers. SALT II was extremely controversial, and the treaty was never actually ratified by the U.S. Senate; in fact, President Carter put it aside when the Soviets invaded Afghanistan in December 1979. In spite of Carter's decision, the terms of the treaty were observed by both sides until President Ronald Reagan bulked up the U.S. arsenal during his presidency.

published in 1983 as a book entitled *Poland: The Role of the Press in Political Change.* She taught herself Polish and visited Poland, where she witnessed the charismatic Solidarity leader Lech Walesa in action.

Albright's professional life was certainly flourishing, but in the beginning of 1982, an event occurred in her personal life that caused a great deal of anguish. One morning, while Joe and Madeleine Albright were sitting in their living room, Joe announced that their marriage was over. Albright has said she will never forget the details of that day. "It was January 13, 1982. At eight o'clock in the morning and sitting on this very chair was Joe Albright, who said to me, 'This marriage is dead and I'm in love with somebody else.'"[14]

The couple had been married for twenty-three years, and Albright has said that she had no indication that her husband was not happy in the relationship. Though the divorce—which was finalized the following year—left her quite comfortable financially, she was stunned and saddened. She took the news very hard. She said, "[My parents] adored each other. . . . They met when they were young and went through nine zillion things together. For me, people stayed married."[15]

Some friends and colleagues have said that Albright changed dramatically in the years following the divorce. They cite the breakup as a crucial turning point in her life. Her good friend Christine Dodson commented, "The divorce gave her time to pursue her career. If Joe had not asked her for a divorce, I am sure she would not have become secretary of state. Instead, she would have been a happy wife, a happy mother."[16]

In an interview on *60 Minutes,* Madeleine Albright spoke to journalist Ed Bradley about the divorce. "I think it made me more self-reliant. . . . I think if it taught me anything, it was to rely on my own judgment and to do what I needed to do for my daughters and for myself."[17]

8

An Influential Democrat

1982–1992

"No nation in the world need be left out of the system we are constructing. . . . We must take advantage of this historic opportunity that now exists to bring the world together in an international system based on democracy, open markets, law and a commitment to peace."

—Madeleine Albright

In 1982, not long after Joe Albright told Madeleine that he wanted a divorce, she entered into another phase of her flourishing and ever-expanding career. Georgetown University's School of Foreign Service appointed her to two positions: Research Professor of International Affairs and Director of Women in Foreign Service Program. Albright's unique background was well suited to the needs of the School of Foreign Service—she brought to the school her superb academic credentials and solid, hands-on experience on Capitol Hill.

This was the job she had been working toward ever since she had first started studying when her twins were born. She tackled the position with the same high degree of diligence, energy, and enthusiasm that she brought to every other phase of her life and career. She may have been distraught about the divorce, but that did not affect her work performance negatively; in fact, it seemed to have aroused in her a new-found sense of determination and ambition.

While at Georgetown, Albright instructed undergraduate and graduate students in international studies, U.S. foreign relations, central and Eastern European politics, and Russian foreign policy. As always, Albright was well prepared for her classes. She was often spotted walking across the Georgetown campus with textbooks and the day's lesson plans under one arm and a folder of newspaper clips from all around the world in another. Albright was a demanding professor, but the students adored her. She was able to translate complex policy concepts in a manner that could be clearly understood, and she also actively engaged her students. She often invited them to her home for weekend retreats, where she led intense discussions about some of the current issues affecting international relations and implemented such techniques as role-playing to help her students understand both sides of an issue. To encourage the young women to prepare for a field that was traditionally dominated by men, Albright instructed them to take on men's roles during these activities.

As director of the Women in Foreign Service program, Albright helped develop programs that created more professional opportunities for women in foreign affairs. She recruited success-ful women in foreign service to give guest lectures; she organized résumé-preparing workshops; and she introduced her students to people who might be able to help them professionally. In the classroom, she taught her women students to assert themselves. She has said, "There are lots of shy people in the world. They don't go anywhere. . . . Women have to learn to interrupt."[1] One of her graduate students, Nancy Soderberg, later said, "Women students have a tendency not to talk, and she made a point of drawing them out." [2]

Albright encountered some antagonism from some of the other professors when she first started teaching at Georgetown. Most of them had published scholarly works, and their primary criticism of her was that she was more interested in politics than in academia. Above all, they complained that she did not have enough teaching experience. Albright admitted, "I wasn't a normal professor. . . . I had worked in government. I hadn't written nine zillion books." [3] Albright's students had an entirely different reaction to her. She became a very popular, beloved campus figure. She drove around Georgetown in a sports car, and she attended nearly every basketball home game. Peter Krogh, the dean of the School of Foreign Service at the time, said, "The students were always with her. She was like a Pied Piper." [4]

Madeleine Albright certainly was interested in politics, and her involvement with the dynamic political community of Washington, D.C., was deepening. In 1981, Georgetown's associate dean, Alan Goodman, came up with the idea to replicate Kissinger's very successful Harvard leadership seminars. Albright helped oversee the establishment of the Georgetown Leadership Seminar, a take-off on Henry Kissinger's brainchild. The weeklong seminar, held in October, attracted intellectuals, bankers, lawyers, businesspeople, and journalists from all over the world. Policy makers from the Pentagon, the State Department, and rising stars in the sphere of international affairs spoke at the conference, and the program became enormously popular and prestigious. Madeleine Albright played a crucial role in the success of the seminar. She spoke on a variety of issues, and her association with the conference vastly expanded her national and international network of contacts.

Albright refined her media skills by participating in a Georgetown-sponsored television program on current affairs.

Broadcast by the Public Broadcasting System and entitled *Great Decisions,* the program was moderated by Dean Krogh. It provided Albright with a forum to spruce up her debating skills and hone her gift of turning complicated information into memorable sound bites. Albright represented the liberal view, Karen Elliot House (a *Wall Street Journal* reporter) was the moderate view, and Richard Allen (Chairman of the Asian Studies Center of the Heritage Foundation) represented the conservative view. It was on this program that Albright developed and then refined her now signature tell-it-like-it-is style. Discussing the Reagan administration's 1983 invasion of Grenada, a small island in the Caribbean, she said, "Of course Grenada worked. It was the Redskins versus the Little Sisters of the Poor, and the score was 101 to nothing."[5] She showcased her forthright, no-nonsense approach to foreign policy on the air as she talked about issues in the Middle East, Central America, Central and Eastern Europe, and Japan. Her confidence grew with each television appearance, and after a while she was granting interviews to foreign television stations. Albright also delivered weekly commentaries for the Voice of America, the U.S.-backed radio station that brings news to U.S. troops abroad and English-speaking listeners around the world.

BACK INTO THE POLITICAL FRAY

While Albright was still teaching at Georgetown, she got back into Democratic Party politics during the 1984 presidential election. She became the foreign policy advisor to Geraldine Ferraro, Democratic candidate Walter Mondale's running mate. Ferraro, the first woman vice-presidential candidate, relied heavily on Albright's advice. Ferraro was charismatic and tough, but she had little experience with foreign policy. Ferraro commented, "[Madeleine Albright] was the perfect teacher. We'd discuss arms control, missile throw weight, geopolitics, you name it. I'd make a tape of the briefings and listen to them again when I was in the bathtub at night."[6] The two women held each other in high regard and formed a strong bond. They were around the same age, they were both mothers, and they shared similar political views. Even after Mondale and Ferraro lost the race, Albright and Ferraro's friendship continued for years.

Albright's love of politics and involvement with others that shared her interest in international affairs rose to astonishing new heights during the 1980s, when she started hosting foreign policy "salons" from her Georgetown home. Over simple dinners, Albright and her guests discussed the hot-button foreign policy issues of the day. The invitees included journalists, politicians, academics, ex-State Department officials, and many of her students. These salons mushroomed into wildly popular gatherings—soon her home became *the* meeting place for Democratic foreign policy makers and other influential Democrats from across the country. Discussions were always lively, and ideas flowed freely. During the Reagan administration, Democrats were, for all intents and purposes, excluded from policymaking. They needed a place to regroup and hash out ideas. One journalist noted, "These were not mere social gatherings, but sessions aimed at laying the groundwork for a Democratic return to power."[7]

The salons really gained steam just before the 1988 presidential campaign when Albright took a leave of absence from Georgetown to serve as senior foreign policy advisor for presidential candidate Michael Dukakis, the governor from Massachusetts. In contrast to the Mondale-Ferraro campaign, when she had spent most of her time giving counsel to the vice-presidential candidate, on this campaign she was advising the presidential candidate himself. Dukakis had practically no experience in the realm of foreign affairs. This put him at a distinct disadvantage because his Republican opponent, George Bush, had been UN ambassador, U.S. envoy to China, and CIA director. Albright had a lot of work to do.

Albright was one of the first people to sign on with Dukakis; she did so even before he announced his candidacy. During the campaign, Albright worked very closely with him—she wrote many of his speeches, articulated his stance on foreign policy matters to the press, and solidified her reputation as a reliable, go-to person on issues related to international relations. He started winning primaries, but after he secured the Democratic nomination, Dukakis's failings as a candidate became abundantly clear. The Bush campaign portrayed Dukakis as an ultra-liberal who lacked a strong vision for the United States, and his public appearances did little to counter that. Albright commented, "his logic, his intellectual honesty, his nuanced approach . . . would have been very interesting in a seminar," but they only hurt him as a presidential candidate.[8]

MICHAEL DUKAKIS

The son of immigrants from Greece, Michael Dukakis attended Swarthmore College and Harvard Law School before he was elected to the Massachusetts House of Representatives as a Democrat in 1963. He was elected governor of Massachusetts and served from 1975 to 1979, then served again from 1983 to 1991. As governor, he initiated an Employment and Training Program to help welfare recipients find employment, overhauled the city's mass transit system, and presided over a period of economic prosperity in the state known as "the Massachusetts miracle." In 1988, Dukakis campaigned for the presidency, with Senator Lloyd Bentsen of Texas as his running mate, emphasizing "competence" over "ideology." Dukakis was painted by Republic opponent George Bush as an extreme liberal—he was attacked from the right for being against the death penalty, for having vetoed a bill requiring schools to start the day with the Pledge of Allegiance, and for allowing weekend furlough for convicted felons. American voters ultimately elected George Bush and running mate Dan Quayle with 54 percent of the vote.

Albright tried to make Dukakis and the Democrats look stronger on national security matters, yet the candidate was unable to convince voters that he could stand up to the Soviet Union should the need arise. Although Dukakis failed in his bid to defeat Bush, Madeleine Albright had firmly established herself as a woman whose opinion mattered.

In 1989, Albright continued to gain influence. Her political career was thriving. In October of that year, she became president of the Center for National Policy, a Washington-based nonprofit research institute formed as a Democratic think tank for the formulation of American foreign policy. An offshoot of the National Endowment for Democracy, the CNP consisted of Democratic leaders in education, industry, and government committed to studying domestic and international policy issues. Albright was dramatically effective in her capacity as president. Her administrative and executive abilities transformed the center into a viable, essential organization. Leon Billings, Ed Muskie's former chief of staff, commented:

> The Center for National Policy was extremely important to Albright. Not only was it a pivotal logical next step in her professional evolution but it gave the Democrats an intellectual policy standing in the foreign relations arena, opposite the Heritage Foundation and AEI. She gave it life.[9]

It was a heady time for foreign policy wonks like Albright. The world was rapidly transforming in the fall of 1989—seismic power shifts abroad were altering the way international relationships were configured. The Berlin Wall, long a symbol of the Iron Curtain that separated the Eastern Communist bloc countries (led by the Soviet Union) from Western democratic countries, was torn down after East Germans took to the streets in protest. In Eastern Europe, Communist regimes were crumbling— a non-Communist government was elected in Poland, and

Czechoslovakia was in the midst of Havel's Velvet Revolution, busily overthrowing the Communist regime installed there. Albright's old friend Jiri Dienstbier, now foreign minister of the new Czech government, invited Albright to visit Prague to witness the exciting transition to democracy. While in her country of birth, Albright met with Havel and advised him on how to set up his office, among other things. When he came to Washington as president of the new Czech Republic, Albright acted as his interpreter, and the two became good friends. In 1990, she traveled to Eastern Europe to help set up educational workshops, organize focus groups, and assist with the transition to democracy. She also monitored elections and gave talks on how to run political campaigns.

Meanwhile, Albright continued to teach at Georgetown, and by then she was more popular than ever. By 1993, senior classes had voted her the most outstanding teacher in the School of Foreign Service four years in a row. By this time, too, she had also improved her reputation as a political scientist. She published three books and several journal articles, and her salons remained the talk of the Democratic community, attracting the brightest minds in the country. On any given night, she never knew who might show up and add to the exciting debate.

Albright befriended scores of Democratic leaders during these gatherings. One night back in 1988, Albright's good friend Chuck Manatt, a leading figure in the Democratic Party, told Albright he would be bringing along a young governor from Arkansas named Bill Clinton. That night, Clinton's intelligence and enthusiasm left an impression on Albright. The talk of the evening ran the gamut from U.S. funding of the Contras in Nicaragua to the nuclear freeze movement to the music of Stan Getz and Dave Brubeck. After the meeting, the two kept in touch. When Clinton asked Albright to write a recommendation for him to the Council of Foreign Relations, she asked him to send her a quick memo outlining his thoughts on foreign

Madeleine Albright speaks at a press conference after president-elect Bill Clinton and vice-president elect Al Gore announced that she was their nomination for ambassador to the United Nations. Albright met Clinton when a mutual acquaintance brought Clinton, then a young Arkansas governor, to one of Albright's salons in her Georgetown home. The two were equally impressed with each other's abilities and Democratic beliefs.

policy. Clinton responded with 120 pages articulating his views; Albright, sufficiently impressed, recommended him.

When Clinton was campaigning for the 1992 presidential election, the charismatic candidate actively sought the advice of the woman whose opinion had become critical to the Democratic community. Albright, with Samuel Berger, Warren Christopher, and Anthony Lake, helped Clinton develop a sound foreign policy platform. When Clinton defeated George Bush in the election in November, ending twelve years of a Republican White House, he pledged to have a diverse cabinet, one that wholly reflected America. Although Clinton asked Albright to head up his transition team for the National Security Council, she was not convinced that he would appoint her to his full-time staff. She was mistaken. At a press conference held on December 22, 1992, President Clinton announced that Madeleine Korbel Albright was his choice for U.S. ambassador to the United Nations.

That day Albright expressed her gratitude not only to Bill Clinton but to the United States and the American people as well. Madeleine Albright had arrived in the United States an eleven-year-old refugee from Czechoslovakia, and after years of tireless study and work, she was one of the most powerful women in government. Not only would she be working closely with the president but she would also be representing her beloved United States around the globe. She later commented, "As a result of the generous spirit of the American people, our family had the privilege growing up as free Americans. You can therefore understand how proud I am to sit at the United Nations behind the nameplate that says 'United States of America.'" [10]

UN Ambassador
1992–1997

"If we have to use force, it is because we are America. We are the indispensable nation. We stand tall. We see further into the future."
—Madeleine Albright

On January 27, 1993, the Senate unanimously confirmed Madeleine Albright as U.S. representative to the United Nations. Sworn into office on the following day, Albright became the second woman to hold the post—the first was Jeane Kirkpatrick, appointed by President Ronald Reagan in 1981.

With this appointment, Albright became the only woman on the fifteen-member Security Council—the most powerful division of the United Nations. The Council is composed of five permanent members (the United States, the United Kingdom, France, China, and Russia) and ten nonpermanent members and is responsible for maintaining world peace and security. At the time, Albright said, "It's a great thrill to represent the United States. . . . And I'm sure that whether you're male or female, you have the same feeling when you are representing the most powerful country in the world."[1] It was indeed thrilling for Albright. As she commented in *Time*, "at this stage in world history, practically every foreign-policy issue has something to do with the UN. It puts me in the wonderful position of being there at the takeoff, during flight and at the landing."[2]

AT THE UNITED NATIONS

Albright moved into the UN ambassador's official residence, a $27,000-a-month apartment suite on the thirty-second floor of the Waldorf-Astoria in New York City, and started her job in February of 1993. She oversaw a staff of a hundred and met with them every Friday to outline the issues of the week. One of the first things she did was organize regular lunches with the other women in the United Nations—there were only seven female representatives at the time.

Albright was an incredibly busy woman. She was not only representing the U.S. government at the UN, but she was also an essential component of President Clinton's advisory team. Clinton had granted Albright's position cabinet-level status. This meant that she would attend biweekly "principals meetings," along with the Secretary of State Warren Christopher, Secretary of Defense William Perry, National Security Advisor Anthony Lake, and the director of the CIA. A member of the National Security Council, Albright became a crucial behind-the-scenes foreign policy strategist and key advisor to the new president.

This arrangement meant that Albright spent a lot of time shuttling back and forth between UN headquarters in New York City and Washington, D.C. The Security Council is likely to meet at anytime, so Albright would often just be landing in New York when she would have to get right back onto a

In her position as UN ambassador for the United States, Albright became a member of Clinton's cabinet and the National Security Council. She had to attend biweekly meetings for key figures in his administration, and would often travel to Washington, D.C., and New York City four or five times a week to fulfill all of her duties. Albright soon developed a public image as no-nonsense official who could handle major world figures with strength and humor.

plane. Sometimes she would travel back and forth between the two cities five times a week. "The people I work with appreciate the fact that I'm plugged into Washington. I'm in the inner circle. I'm involved in everything," she once stated in her characteristically blunt style.[3]

Madeleine Albright soon became a visible personality in the news, known just as much for her no-nonsense manner as for her sense of humor and snappy one-liners. For example, when a representative from Burma insisted that his government wasn't guilty of human rights violations, he said to Albright, "You can see that the people are smiling here." Albright retorted, "I had a lot of friends in Czechoslovakia who used to smile, but only because they were scared."[4] By this time, she had become adroit at using the media to her advantage—she understood that the press was an invaluable tool in informing the public and attempting to curry their favor. She once called the Cable News Network (CNN) "the sixteenth member of the Security Council."[5] One of Albright's missions in her new position was to build support for the UN among Americans—she wanted to educate them about the valuable role the international organization plays in world affairs. She traveled around the country, speaking to audiences about the UN and foreign policy.

In the 1980s, many people in Congress believed that the UN had grown too expensive and powerful and that the United States should not have to continue to financially support it. The United States owed the UN millions of dollars in unpaid dues when Albright became an ambassador; it became her personal crusade to convince Congress to pay the long-delinquent dues. She said:

> I do not believe I can fulfill my mission to the UN unless I am able to persuade the American people of the importance of the mission. Yes, it costs money to help keep peace around the world. But by any measure, the most expensive peacekeeping mission is a bargain compared to the least expensive war—not just because it costs fewer dollars, but because it costs fewer lives, creating fewer orphans and refugees, and because it plants the seeds of future reconciliation.[6]

Albright got straight to work at building international connections, going above and beyond the typical duties of a UN ambassador. She visited more than two dozen countries, including Cambodia, Mozambique, the Sudan, Somalia, Ethiopia, Bosnia, Croatia, Slovenia, Moldova, Armenia, Azerbaijan, El Salvador, and Haiti. There, she monitored peacekeeping operations and other UN activities. This steady stream of visits to heads of state was unprecedented for a UN ambassador, but Albright was an entirely different breed from her predecessors.

From the beginning of her tenure as ambassador, Madeleine Albright made it clear that she was a formidable presence, a leader with a strong vision of the role that the UN

ALBRIGHT, JESSE HELMS, AND THE U.S. DEBT TO THE UN

In the 1980s, Republicans in Congress began to call for a reduction in the U.S. share of the United Nations' budget. They argued that the UN had become too expensive and that it was no longer in the best interests of the United States to continue financing the organization. Consequently, the government let payments lapse. In the 1990s, Senator Jesse Helms, the Republican leader of the U.S. Senate Committee on Foreign Relations, continued to speak out against the UN; by this time, the United States owed the UN about $1 billion. When Albright became U.S. ambassador to the UN, she lobbied Congress several times to pay those back dues. She even cultivated a close relationship with the controversial, ultraconservative Senator Helms—she toured his home state, delivered a lecture at his alma mater, and even gave him a T-shirt that read "Somebody at the State Department Loves Me." Albright came up with a plan to pay off the debt, decrease the U.S. share of the UN budget, and reconfigure the UN bureaucratic system.

It was not until 1999 that the Senate finally approved legislation related to the issue. The measure, approved 98 to 1, reduced the U.S. share from 25 percent to 20 percent, and also cut back on the amount the United States contributed to UN peacekeeping operations from 31 percent to 25 percent. Madeleine Albright, who was by then secretary of state, agreed to support the cut; Jesse Helms accepted the compromise as well, agreeing not to press for the more radical changes within the UN he had originally demanded.

should play. As writer Thomas Blood noted, Albright was just as clear in her belief that the United States has an obligation to uphold its responsibility as the only democratic superpower. She said, "Neither our history, nor our character, nor our self-interest will allow us to withdraw from the center stage of global, political, and economic life."[7] Albright never held back from expressing her views of how the United States should behave in the international arena. One Washington insider once said, "When Madeleine sits at the table, she is very often the voice of conscience saying we *should* do this or we *should* do that."[8]

During her first few years as ambassador, Albright championed what she called "assertive multilateralism," the practice of joining U.S. forces with those of the United Nations to maintain peace abroad. Albright was particularly adamant about taking a firm stand against the tyrants of the world. Her family's experience with the Nazis had left an indelible mark on her, and she was determined not to let history repeat itself. For this reason, she consistently worked to end the persecution of innocent people at all costs, even if it meant using military force. She explained by saying, "My mindset is Munich. Most of my generation's is Vietnam."[9] By this she meant that she had first-hand experience with the horrible consequences of the policy of appeasement—the Munich Pact had essentially paved the way for Hitler and the Nazis to take over Czechoslovakia and move into the rest of Europe. Albright was insistent that this not happen again, and she developed a tough, hawkish reputation, never hesitating to advocate military intervention.

HAITI AND IRAQ

One of Albright's greatest successes during her tenure as ambassador was her courageous role in persuading the UN to endorse the U.S. invasion of Haiti. In 1991, military leaders had overthrown the government of the democratically

One of Albright's most outstanding accomplishments as the UN ambassador was her ability to persuade the United Nations to endorse the U.S. invasion of Haiti. Albright met with council members individually to encourage them to back the United States. Her hard work paid off; on July 31, 1994, the Security Council approved UN Resolution 940, permitting the U.S. invasion.

elected Haitian president Jean-Bertrand Aristide. By the summer of 1994, the impoverished Caribbean country was in a state of chaos: The military was rounding up dissenters and throwing them into prison; other Haitians crowded into overfilled boats bound for Florida. Many drowned.

At a 1994 UN Security Council meeting, Albright declared "They have created a puppet show and called it a government." [10] While the State Department and the chairman of the Joint Chiefs of Staff, General Colin Powell, thought that it would be fruitless to try to seek Security Council approval for military intervention in Haiti, Albright believed she could win the council's support. When she said to the president, "If you give me the go-ahead, I think I can get the votes," he told her to give it a try.[11] Albright met with each of the council representatives, and on July 31, 1994, the Security Council approved UN Resolution 940, allowing the United States to lead an invasion into Haiti to unseat the military dictatorship. Immediately after the resolution was passed, Albright gave the Haitian military leaders an ultimatum, "You can depart voluntarily and soon, or you can depart involuntarily and soon."[12] On October 15, 1994, President Aristide and his government were restored to power.

Albright's effectiveness was astounding. Some point to her charm and some point to her forcefulness; others maintain that it is her command of the facts and her preparedness that make her so exceptionally capable. Yuli Vorontsov, Russia's representative on the Security Council at the time, remarked about the Haiti resolution, "It was [Madeleine Albright's] logic, not her charm, that changed my mind. She is very effective."[13]

Albright's maneuverings to keep the trade embargo against Iraq in place was another example of the lengths that she would go to take a stand against dictatorships. In 1990, after Iraqi dictator Saddam Hussein invaded neighboring Kuwait, the UN imposed heavy economic sanctions against Iraq. The intention was to try to force the Iraqi leader to surrender his chemical and biological weapons and missiles and to stop him from threatening his neighbors. A U.S.-led coalition drove the Iraqi army from Kuwait and a cease-fire was negotiated. Saddam, however, continued to violate UN terms. In 1994, France, Russia, and China proposed that the UN relax its sanctions because Iraqi civilians were dying of malnutrition and disease because they were unable to procure medical supplies and food. Ambassador Albright felt strongly that the sanctions should be kept in place because Saddam Hussein was hiding weapons the international community considered illegal. She said, "Those sanctions have worked. . . . In imposing sanctions, we had no wish to hurt the Iraqi people. We exempted food and medicine and offered Saddam Hussein a chance to sell oil to buy additional humanitarian supplies."[14] Defying protocol, Albright flew to the capitals of the Security Council countries to show the heads of state the secret photos (taken by the CIA) of the stashes of weapons the Iraqi dictator had been hiding. The motion to relax the sanctions was eventually dropped.

Albright was focused like a laser beam on getting the job done, but she became a very controversial figure. Her hawkish sensibilities struck many as reckless and blindly idealistic, and her disregard for standard bureaucratic procedure brought sharp criticism from Albright's detractors. Normally, ambassadors consult with their fellow ambassadors on the council—Albright angered some of her colleagues on the Security Council by going over their heads. She once even told the defense minister from France to mind his own business. She had carved out a reputation for herself as a tough woman, yet she also had a sense of humor about herself. When an Iraqi newspaper called her a serpent, she began to wear serpent-shaped brooches. When someone else called her witch, even going so far as sending her a broom, she displayed the broom proudly in her office. Throughout the criticism and controversies, Albright never compromised her ideals, and she continued to serve the president and his administration in the ways she thought best.

THE BALKAN CRISIS AND SOMALIA

By the time Bill Clinton entered the White House, the civil war in Bosnia—part of the former Yugoslavia—had already been responsible for the deaths of thousands of innocent people. When Communist governments collapsed and Bosnia declared its independence from Yugoslavia in 1992, Bosnian Serbs and Croats tried to force Bosnian Muslims out of their territory. The Serbs attacked cities where Muslims lived and executed them. The horrific "ethnic cleansing" and the concentration camps established in the area were frighteningly reminiscent of the Holocaust.

The UN had initiated a relief effort to assist the Muslims, and the United States had airdropped some supplies to the victims, but Madeleine Albright believed that stronger action was needed. She was once again acting on her belief that the United States, as a democratic superpower, had a duty to stand up to aggression. In August 1993, she wrote a memo to President Clinton recommending that the United States lead NATO in launching air strikes on strategic military targets in Bosnia.

Later that year, the issue of whether or not the United States should intervene in Bosnia was beginning to weigh on the Clinton administration, and opinions within the circle of the president's closest advisors clashed. Colin Powell, the chairman of the Joint Chiefs of Staff, was determined to prevent Clinton from launching air strikes. He felt that the strikes would be ineffective and that too many American ground troops would be needed to achieve the peace. Powell believed that the United States should get involved in the crises of other countries militarily only if there was a clear, defined goal that was achievable through military action. Albright and Powell argued openly about this issue. At one point she even said, "What's the point of having this superb military that you're always talking about if we can't use it?" Powell was shocked. He described his reaction in his autobiography: "I thought I would have an aneurysm. American GIs were not toy soldiers to be moved around on some sort of global gameboard." [15] By this time, Albright's reputation as a hawk was solidified in the eyes of political observers in the United States and abroad.

One of the most controversial military actions that Albright was involved with during her time with the UN was the U.S. effort to stop the fighting in the African nation of Somalia. After a group of rebels overthrew the government in the tiny country, thousands of Somalis were dying every day from malnutrition and disease. There was a devastating drought, and rival clans ruthlessly fought one another in what became a full-blown civil war. Innocent Somalis fled to the cities, which quickly became swollen with the refugees. The Red Cross sent in people to help the starving and sick, but they were unable to make a serious dent in alleviating the problem as gangs of thieves were plundering supplies. In December 1992, at the end of his tenure in the White House, President Bush had sent troops to assist the relief effort. The goal of the U.S. troops was to establish open food and aid routes so Somalis could get the supplies that they needed; then UN forces would take control of the operations.

On March 26, 1993, the Security Council passed a unanimous resolution that would replace the U.S. forces with UN troops. Unfortunately, the fighting had intensified by that point, and American troops couldn't easily pull out. On June 5, a group of rebels led by warlord Muhammad Farah Aidid ambushed and killed twenty-three Pakistani soldiers, troops that were part of the UN peacekeeping force. Although most Americans felt that the U.S. mission was over and it was time for the U.S. soldiers to come home, disaster struck. In an abortive attempt to capture Aidid, four American soldiers were killed. Angered and upset, American civilians continued to question the U.S. military presence in Somalia, but Madeleine Albright defended it. She felt that Aidid had to be stopped, and she blamed him for the deaths of the U.S. troops and the UN peacekeepers. In October 1993, the situation took a turn for the worse when Somali forces shot down three helicopters. Eighteen American soldiers were killed, and an angry Somali mob dragged the body of a U.S. soldier through the streets of Mogadishu, the capital city. Americans watched in shock and horror when the gruesome footage was shown on television and reacted with anger and sadness as Somalis burned American flags.

Americans wondered why and how such an awful thing could have happened and why the mission in Somalia had changed. Some blamed the UN; the UN secretary-general, Boutros Boutros-Ghali, blamed the United States. Others pointed fingers at Madeleine Albright. Somehow Albright seemed to be shouldering most of the blame, although in reality, as Warren Christopher has said, "Madeleine had absolutely nothing to do with Somalia."[16] Regardless of who was at fault, it was a sobering experience for all involved. This is when Albright began reconfiguring her approach to international affairs. Her new policy, coined the "do-ability doctrine," stressed that each international problem had to be assessed and treated separately. This was a distinct departure from the "assertive multilaterism" that she had initially advocated.

TOUGH-TALKING ALBRIGHT

Throughout her four years as ambassador, Albright continued to be dogged by criticism. During an interview, correspondent Barbara Walters once asked Albright how she felt about being criticized so often. "Do you care?" Walters asked. "No," Albright responded.[17] After Albright spoke out against Serbian aggression and supported the establishment of a Bosnian War Crimes Tribunal to investigate the atrocities committed by the Serbs, she took a trip to Bosnia to see for herself what was happening. Protesters pelted stones and screamed obscenities at her and her aides. One day, while Albright was walking outside the United Nations in New York, a woman shouted at her, "Why are you so awful to the Serbs?" Albright responded to the woman in Serbo-Croatian, "Because *they are* awful."[18]

Albright's tough talk and tough stance continued to generate controversy throughout her tenure as UN ambassador.

Other people loved her style and appreciated her bluntness and verve, perhaps none more so than the president himself.

In February of 1996, Cuban fighter pilots gunned down two unarmed civilian planes flown by members of a group called Brothers to the Rescue, a group of exiles that protested against Fidel Castro's Communist government. The planes were in international airspace, so the action infuriated Cuban exiles and many Americans. Albright listened to a taped conversation of the pilots bragging about their bravery. They used the Spanish word *cojones*, a term which suggests virility, to boast about their courage. Albright commented to the press, "Frankly, this is not cojones, this is cowardice." Although some delegates to the United Nations were bothered by the comment, considering it vulgar and inappropriate, President Clinton loved it. He said it was "probably the most effective one-liner in the whole administration's foreign policy." [19]

Albright never let the criticism interfere with her duty. When she participated in the 1995 Fourth World Conference on Women in Beijing, China, she was lambasted for attending. Many people had encouraged her not to attend the event. Conservatives viewed the conference as a forum for the endorsement of birth control and abortion; liberals thought she should boycott the conference because of China's dreadful history of human rights abuses. Albright, however, firmly believed that the United States' participation was essential, and she proudly led the U.S. delegation to the conference.

By 1996, President Clinton had been elected to another term. When Secretary of State Warren Christopher announced his retirement, the president immediately turned to Madeleine Albright. Clinton respected and admired her approach to foreign affairs. He greatly appreciated her energy and her loyalty, and she had more than proven herself to be an effective communicator and staunch defender of U.S. interests.

Although Madeleine Albright was a controversial figure and had been heavily criticized, her appointment to the position of secretary of state was unanimously confirmed. On January 23, 1997, in a swearing-in ceremony attended by all three of her daughters, Albright became the highest-ranking woman in government in the history of the United States.

10

Madam Secretary
1997–2000

"I have been a woman for 60 years. I have only been Secretary of State for a short time, so we're still seeing how the two go together. My appointment does show the incredible opportunity in this country, and representing the most powerful country in the world [is] a great challenge and an honor."

—Madeleine Albright

During Madeleine Albright's swearing-in ceremony on January 23, 1997, President Clinton said in his comments that her gender had nothing to do with her getting the position. He did say, however, "Am I proud that I got a chance to appoint the first woman secretary of state? You bet I am. My mamma's smiling down at me right now." At the event, Madeleine also offered up another of her memorable one-liners. During the ceremonies, the new secretary of state turned to her predecessor

President Clinton, shaking Madeleine Albright's hand after she had been sworn in as the first woman secretary of state, firmly denied that Albright's gender factored in to her being chosen the for the position. Clinton maintained that he had hired the person with the best combination of qualities, though he was proud to be the president to appoint the highest-ranking woman in the history of the U.S. government.

Warren Christopher and commented, "I can only hope that my heels can fill your shoes."[1]

When Albright started her term in 1997, she faced an array of prickly international situations. Among those problems were the collapse of the peace in the Middle East; Russia's opposition to the proposed expansion of NATO; a troublesome relationship with China; and the fighting in the former Yugoslavia.

After she settled into her new office (she found that the marble bathroom had been clearly set up for men and there were suit racks and columns of sock drawers), Albright threw herself into her new position with gusto. One of her first meetings was held with President Clinton and the new secretary-general of the United Nations, Kofi Annan. President Clinton and Congressional members were not happy with the role that the previous secretary-general, Boutros-Ghali, had played in the Somalia missions, and Albright had butted heads with him about Bosnia and other matters. As UN ambassador, she had maneuvered to convince her colleagues not to reelect him. This was hailed by many as a huge success; but others perceived it as a manifestation of her overly aggressive, even bullying, ways.

In March, Albright set off on a whirlwind tour, meeting with the dignitaries of nine major world capitals. Not only was she establishing contacts with these heads of state, but she was also beginning to tackle some of her most pressing concerns. In Rome, she met with Romano Prodi, the prime minister of Italy who, like Albright, favored the expansion of NATO. In Russia, she met with Foreign Minister Yevgeny Primakov and President Boris Yeltsin, in preparation for a summit between Presidents Clinton and Yeltsin to be held later that month. She visited South Korea and then Beijing, China. With Chinese leaders she discussed Communist North Korea's nuclear weapons and the issue of Hong Kong, which was going to be transferred from British rule to Communist China on July 1, 1997. Long a fierce advocate of international human rights, Albright was also very candid with the Chinese about how the United States viewed their terrible human rights record.

The trip was a resounding success, and it definitively announced her arrival in the international arena. The leaders responded well to the new secretary of state, admiring her seemingly boundless enthusiasm, grasp of the facts, and forthright approach. The American press and public were also dazzled by Albright—during her first months of her new position, she was surrounded by a flurry of reporters.

A STARTLING REVELATION

One of those reporters, Michael Dobbs of the *Washington Post,* was doing some research on Albright's early life when he came across some startling information. Dobbs had talked to Albright's cousin Dagmar, who revealed that Albright's family were not Catholics, and were, in fact, Czech Jews. The reporter also discovered a long essay that Mandula Korbel had written about her family's escape from Prague in 1939—Mandula had written it after Josef died in 1977 but had never shown it to her children. As he continued his investigation, Dobbs also found out that three of Albright's grandparents had perished in Hitler's concentration camps.

When Dobbs told Albright about his findings, she reacted with shock. She said, "This obviously was a major surprise to me. I had never been told this."[2] Albright did not want to discuss this part of her past, considering it a private matter. She said she needed time to process the information and investigate it on her own. She said, "I thought that the right way to do this would be to check it out and then have a family discussion."[3] When the story came out, it created quite a stir. Many reporters and pundits speculated that Albright had always known the truth about her past and had kept it hidden so it wouldn't interfere with her career. Some believed that Albright had not in fact known (her friends and family support this view) but wondered why her parents had kept the truth from their children. Others expressed surprise that Albright had been so ignorant of her own history. Because of the way the story was revealed to her and because of press reaction and speculation, Albright was furious. Her biographer, Ann Blackman wrote, "The harsh way in which she learned the news, and the second-guessing of her parents' motives, infuriated her. 'I went from being sad to sick to mad,' [Albright] says."[4] While the press was asking all of these questions, Albright was struggling herself to figure out why her parents had withheld the truth from her. In spite of her questions, she said, "I believe my parents did wonderful things for us."[5]

A few months later, Albright was invited by Czech president Václav Havel to come to Prague so he could bestow on her the Czech Republic's country's highest honor, the Order of the White Lion. Albright made an emotional visit to Prague, where she went to Pinkas Synagogue in Prague and saw for herself the names of her grandparents—Olga and Arnost Körbel—on a memorial to Holocaust victims. She also toured the old Jewish cemetery and visited the Terezin ghetto and her grandfather's town. In her remarks to the press that day, she said:

> As I stood looking at that melancholy wall, all the walls, I not only grieved for those members of my family whose names are inscribed here, but I also thought about my parents. I thought about the choices they made. They clearly confronted the most excruciating decision a human being can face when they left members of their family behind, even as they saved me from certain death.[6]

GETTING DOWN TO BUSINESS

For a brief time, Albright was consumed with the issue of her family history, but she soon managed to shift the focus back to her duties as secretary of state. Albright had pledged to make more Americans understand the relevance of foreign policy in their lives, and she made a concerted effort to do so. In her first year in office alone she made nineteen trips to speak on this issue. During one of these speaking engagements, she said to a group of high school students in Texas, "Not only can foreign policy be cool, it can be awesome."[7] She elicited positive reactions from many of her audiences, but she did encounter some difficulty during an event at Ohio State University in February 1998, an event televised by CNN. While Albright was trying to explain U.S. policy on Iraq to the audience, she was drowned out by a group chanting, "One, two, three, four, we don't want your racist war." One man confronted Albright about the fact that Iraqi citizens would be murdered during a proposed bombing campaign in Iraq. He asked her how she could sleep at night. Albright, taken aback, responded sharply, "What we are doing is so that all of you can sleep tonight."[8] Critics commented that she had not handled the situation very well.

Regardless of the criticism directed at her and her policies, Albright's engagement with her job was such that she became something of a celebrity at the beginning of her stint as head of the State Department. She was highly visible in the media, especially on CNN. She was acclaimed for her sense of fun and her sense of humor, but she was probably most admired for her dedication to her job and her country. Albright had made some major achievements by the end of her first year as secretary of state.

For example, she successfully pressed for the Senate's ratification of the Chemical Weapons Treaty. This treaty, developed in the 1980s during the Reagan era and signed by President George Bush, aimed to forbid the manufacture or purchase of chemical weapons by any nation. By 1997, 160 nations had signed it, but the United States, Libya, and Iraq had not. Conservative members of Congress strongly opposed it, arguing that Libya and Iraq, because of their poor behavior in the past, might use such weapons against the United States; they believed that the United States should maintain the capacity to respond accordingly. Senator Jesse Helms expressed concern about the accord, but Madeleine Albright's close relationship with the conservative senator helped the treaty get signed into law in April 1997.

To win Senator Helms' support, Albright seriously considered his plan to streamline the overly bureaucratic U.S. foreign policy system. Based on his blueprint, Albright came up with her own version. That same month, the president approved the incorporation of the Arms Control and Disarmament Agency and the U.S. Information Agency into the State Department. As a result, the State Department was allotted a larger budget and granted more authority.

Another one of Albright's successes was helping to facilitate the expansion of NATO. From the beginning of his first term, President Clinton had supported the expansion of NATO to include the Czech Republic, Poland, and Hungary, all former

Soviet bloc countries. He firmly believed that the incorporation of these Eastern European nations into NATO would bolster America's long-term relationship with all of Europe. He felt that it was essential to maintaining stability in the region. At a NATO summit in July 1996, Ambassador Albright had said, "The purpose of enlargement is to do for Europe's east what NATO did fifty years ago for Europe's west: to integrate new democracies, defeat old hatreds, provide confidence in economic recovery, and deter conflict."[9]

Clinton and Albright encountered some opposition from Russia on this issue. After all, NATO was initially established to protect Western Europe from the Soviets. Albright handled the situation deftly. During a visit to Moscow, she did her utmost to allay the Russians' fears. She explained that the West was proposing a new limit on conventional weapons in Europe, which could reduce the U.S. stockpile of aircraft, artillery, and tanks by almost fifty percent. She also proposed a special Russia-NATO council with its own permanent secretariat. Ultimately, the Russians accepted the expansion, albeit skeptically. So, in July 1997, Hungary, the Czech Republic, and Poland were all formally invited to become a part of NATO, and by March 1999, all three countries had voted to join. It was an accomplishment of which Albright was especially proud.

THE MIDDLE EAST

One of the criticisms leveled at Madeleine Albright at the beginning of her tenure as secretary of state was that she seemed to stay away from the seriously contentious issues of the time, particularly the Arab-Israeli conflict. Indeed, one of the greatest challenges of her term with the Clinton administration was the crisis in the Middle East.

In 1995, Israel's Prime Minister, Yitzhak Rabin, and PLO leader Yasser Arafat, aided by Madeleine Albright and Warren Christopher, had taken tremendous strides toward peace, but then an Israeli man opposed to Rabin's policies shot and killed the prime minister. After that, the violence intensified—clashes continued between Palestinians and Jewish settlers; extremist Palestinian groups claimed responsibility for suicide bombings that murdered several Israelis. Albright had not returned to the region since Rabin's murder. In fall 1997, however, Albright made her first official trip to the Middle East as secretary of state. Her mission was to try to bring peace to the war-torn region. Recalling how the previous effort at peace had failed, Albright worked hard to try to bring the two current leaders—Israeli Prime Minister Benjamin Netanyahu and PLO leader Yasser Arafat—to a compromise. She was tough on both sides, emphasizing that both bore the responsibility of honoring the peace process. After three grueling days, Albright left the region frustrated, calling her visit a failure. She resolutely declared, "I will come back here when the leaders are ready to make the hard decisions. I will not come back to tread water."[10]

By December 1999, Ehud Barak, the new Israeli prime minister, seemed more willing to negotiate than his predecessor, and by 2000, much of Secretary of State Albright's attention was focused on the Middle East. In June of that year, when there had been a particularly bloody outbreak of attacks, she met separately with Arafat and Barak to try to push the negotiations forward. "There is no higher foreign policy priority for the Clinton administration than an Israeli-Palestinian peace," she declared.

KOSOVO

Secretary of State Albright also had to confront the volatile situation in the troubled areas of the former Yugoslavia. When a movement to form an independent Kosovar state (free from Serbian rule) had started to gain momentum, Serbian leader Slobodan Milošević and his troops invaded the province of Kosovo and a ruthless campaign of "ethnic cleansing" ensued. Serbian troops murdered innocent ethnic Albanians, while forcing others to leave their homes and flee the country. In September 1998, Albright and Russian foreign minister Igor Ivanov called on Milošević to put a stop to the bloodshed and negotiate with the Kosovars. They drew up a proposal granting Kosovo considerable autonomy, but Milošević rejected it and even stepped up his horrific campaign. Despite more repeated warnings from NATO, Serb forces continued the genocide.

Madeleine Albright felt that Slobodan Milošević could be stopped only by force, and she pressed hard for NATO-backed air strikes. On March 23, 1999, NATO began its air campaign, focusing initially on military sites but gradually expanding its targets to include some infrastructure.

Albright endured a lot of criticism for her aggressive and vociferous support of using military force, but in June, Milošević conceded defeat. He signed an agreement that resulted in the end of the bombing campaign, the withdrawal of Serbian forces, and the entrance of NATO peacekeeping troops into the region.

IRAQ

Secretary of State Albright also took the hardline approach against Iraqi dictator Saddam Hussein. After the Gulf War in 1991, the UN had passed several resolutions demanding that Iraq stop the production and use of weapons of mass destruction—chemical, biological, and nuclear weaponry. Iraq continually refused to cooperate fully with the UN weapons inspectors. Iraqi soldiers even physically prevented inspectors from accessing potential storage sites. By 1997, President Clinton had grown wary and expressed concern about Iraq's failure to disarm. At the end of that year, a team of UN inspectors was in Iraq, when Hussein suddenly demanded that all of the American inspectors leave the country. The UN agreed to pull all of the inspectors out of the country until a diplomatic solution could be reached. Although President Clinton prepared to send in military forces, he also advocated a diplomatic solution to the problem.

Meanwhile, Secretary of State Albright spent a great deal of her time speaking out against Saddam Hussein and trying to drum up support from European and Middle Eastern allies in case military force had to be used against the Iraqi dictator. She once wrote in a *Newsweek* article, "Why do we care so much about access for weapons inspectors? Because Saddam has a long track record of aggression and deception. Unlike any other modern leader, he has used chemical weapons against other countries and even against his own people."

Saddam Hussein continued to be uncooperative. In January 1998, he said he would not work with UN inspectors unless the sanctions against Iraq were lifted. He also accused one of the American inspectors of being a spy. President Clinton

ALBRIGHT'S VISIT TO NORTH KOREA

By the end of 2000, Madeleine Albright had made history again when she met with North Korean leader Kim Jong II. She was the first U.S. secretary of state and the highest-ranking official ever to visit the country. The two discussed ways the United States and North Korea could improve their ties, and set the stage for President Clinton's possible visit to the North Korean capital, Pyongyang.

Although the threat of war has been looming over the Korean Peninsula since the end of the Korean War, there were some renewed concerns about North Korea's long-range missile development program and its export of missiles to Iran and Syria. The country was also on the U.S. list of countries supporting international terrorism. Secretary of State Albright wanted to meet North Korea's notoriously reclusive leader and assess if he was serious about improving his country's relations with the United States and its allies in East Asia. Albright and Clinton hoped to convince North Korea to abandon its missile program, while North Korea, suffering for years from food shortage and an economic crisis, viewed improved relations with the West as the best way to return to prosperity without sacrificing power.

responded by bolstering U.S. forces in the Persian Gulf area. Domestically and internationally, Secretary of State Albright continued to try to rally support for a war on Iraq, but she met with resistance from many sides. In February 1998, UN Secretary-General Kofi Annan met with Saddam Hussein and brokered a deal that would allow inspectors to return to Iraq, but that summer, Hussein again refused to cooperate. He continued to do so until March 2003, when President George W. Bush and his "coalition of the willing" launched a controversial war against the dictator and his government, calling for a "regime change."

CITIZEN ALBRIGHT

Albright ardently continued to defend American interests abroad and stayed true to her decidedly pro-American stance throughout her four years as secretary of state. "I truly do believe in the goodness of American power," she said to Nancy Gibbs of *Time*. "I don't just mean military force. I mean the role the U.S. can have in the world when it's properly used." [11]

After leaving office in January 2001, when Republican George W. Bush became president, Albright returned to Georgetown as a professor. Today, as head of The Albright Group, LLC, she remains actively involved in international affairs, advising multinational companies and organizations about health, the environment, and foreign policy issues. As chair of the board of the National Democratic Institute for International Affairs, she continues to promote and assist democratization efforts around the globe. With her direct, no-nonsense approach to foreign policy, and her remarkable ability to charm and appeal to different types of people, Albright has managed to win the admiration and support of powerful leaders across the political spectrum. Her integrity, conviction, and clarity have helped Americans care about foreign policy again.

Growing up in an era when few women were even encouraged to work, Madeleine Albright—through sheer hard work

Today, Madeleine Albright works with the company she founded, The Albright Group, LCC, a global strategy firm, to give others the benefit of her great experience and knowledge in foreign policy and international affairs. She also writes numerous articles for current events magazines and even wrote an autobiography, *Madam Secretary*.

and determination—defied the odds. She successfully entered the traditionally male-dominated world of foreign policy, paving the way for other women to follow. Madeleine Albright's journey from a Czech refugee to the highest-ranking woman in the United States government is truly a remarkable one. As President Clinton once said, "Madeleine Albright embodies the best of America. It says something about our country . . . that a young girl raised in the shadow of Nazi aggression in Czechoslovakia can rise to the highest diplomatic office in America."[12]

Chronology

1937 Marie (Madeleine) Jana Körbel is born in Prague, Czechoslovakia, to Josef and Mandula Körbel.

1939 The Körbel family flees to England after German Nazis invade Czechoslovakia.

1945 The Körbels return to Czechoslovakia when World War II ends; they learn that their entire family has been slaughtered by the Nazis (Madeleine is not told).

1947 Madeleine attends boarding school in Switzerland.

1948 Mandula Korbel and her children (Madeleine, Katherine, and John) escape to the United States after a political coup in Czechoslovakia; Josef joins them later.

1949 The Korbels move to Colorado; Josef accepts a teaching position at the University of Denver.

1955 Madeleine graduates from Kent School for Girls.

1959 Madeleine graduates from Wellesley College and marries Joseph Medill Patterson Albright.

1961 Twin daughters Anne and Alice are born. Madeleine enrolls in graduate program for political science at Columbia University while Joseph works for *Newsday*.

1967 Daughter Katherine is born.

1968 Madeleine Albright earns master's degree in political science and moves to Washington, D.C., when Joseph becomes head of *Newsday*'s Washington Bureau.

1972 She is elected Chairman of the Board of the Beauvoir School.

1976 She receives her doctorate and becomes chief legislative assistant to Senator Edmund M. Muskie.

1977 Josef Korbel dies.

1978 Albright becomes congressional liaison for the National Security Council under President Jimmy Carter.

1981 Albright is awarded fellowships from the center for Strategic and International Studies and from the Woodrow Wilson International Center for Scholars at the Smithsonian Institution.

1982 Albright becomes research professor of International Affairs and Director of Women in Foreign Service Program at Georgetown University School of Foreign Service, where she serves for eleven years. Joseph and Madeleine Albright are divorced.

1984 Albright becomes foreign policy advisor to Geraldine Ferraro for the 1984 presidential election.

1988 Albright works on Michael Dukakis' presidential campaign as foreign policy coordinator. Around this time her foreign policy "salons," run from her Georgetown home, become enormously popular.

1989 Albright becomes president of Center for National Policy. Mandula Korbel dies.

1992 Albright helps devise Democratic platform for the upcoming election with Democratic National Committee.

1993 President Clinton names Albright U.S. ambassador to the United Nations.

1997 Albright is appointed secretary of state of the United States, the first woman to hold the position. She learns that she was born Jewish, not Catholic as she had been raised, and that her three grandparents perished in the Holocaust. She helps push through the ratification of the Chemical Weapons Treaty.

1999 NATO expands to include Hungary, Poland, and the Czech Republic; in March NATO launches strikes on Slobodan Milošević's Serb targets in Kosovo; three months later Milošević concedes defeat.

2000 Madeleine Albright meets with North Korean leader Kim Jong Il.

2001 Albright forms The Albright Group, LLC, a global strategy consulting firm.

2003 *Madam Secretary*, Madeleine Albright's autobiography, is published by Miramax Books.

Notes

CHAPTER 2

1. Ann Blackman, *Seasons of Her Life: A Biography of Madeleine K. Albright.* New York: Scribner, 1998, p. 26.

2. Michael Dobbs, *Madeleine Albright: A Twentieth-Century Odyssey.* New York: Henry Holt, 1999, p. 24.

3. Ibid., p. 25.

4. Blackman, *Seasons of Her Life: A Biography of Madeleine K. Albright,* p. 26.

CHAPTER 3

1. Dobbs, *Madeleine Albright: A Twentieth-Century Odyssey,* p. 32.

2. Ibid., p. 34.

3. Ibid., p. 39.

4. Blackman, *Seasons of Her Life: A Biography of Madeleine K. Albright,* p. 36.

5. Dobbs, *Madeleine Albright: A Twentieth-Century Odyssey,* p. 28.

6. Ibid., p. 43.

7. Blackman, *Seasons of Her Life: A Biography of Madeleine K. Albright,* p. 39.

8. Molly Sinclair, "Woman on Top of the World," *The Washington Post,* January 6, 1991, p. F4.

9. Blackman, *Seasons of Her Life: A Biography of Madeleine K. Albright,* p. 42.

10. Nancy Gibbs, "The Many Lives of Madeleine," p. 58.

11. Blackman, *Seasons of Her Life: A Biography of Madeleine K. Albright,* p. 55.

12. Ibid., p. 45.

13. Jeremy Byman, *Madam Secretary: The Story of Madeleine Albright.* Greensboro, N.C.: Morgan Reynolds, p. 19.

14. Ibid., p. 20.

CHAPTER 4

1. Lally Weymouth. "'As I Find Out More, I'm Very Proud': An Exclusive Interview with Madeleine Albright." *Newsweek,* February 24, 1997, p. 30.

2. Blackman, *Seasons of Her Life: A Biography of Madeleine K. Albright,* p. 66.

3. Ibid., p. 71.

4. Ibid., p. 73.

5. Madeleine Albright, "Message from the Secretary of State," *The Mini Page,* March 17, 1996, p. 4

6. Dobbs, *Madeleine Albright: A Twentieth-Century Odyssey,* p.119.

7. Blackman, *Seasons of Her Life: A Biography of Madeleine K. Albright,* p. 83.

8. Ibid., p. 85.

CHAPTER 5

1. Thomas Blood, *Madam Secretary: A Biography of Madeleine Albright.* New York: St. Martin's Press, 1997, p. 172.

2. Michael Dobbs and John M. Goshko, "Albright's Personal Odyssey Shaped Foreign Policy Beliefs." *The Washington Post,* December 6, 1996, p. A64.

3. Blackman, *Seasons of Her Life: A Biography of Madeleine K. Albright,* p. 84.

4. Albright, "Message from the Secretary of State," p. 4.

5. Gibbs, "The Many Lives of Madeleine," p. 58.

6. Blood, *Madam Secretary: A Biography of Madeleine Albright*, p. 236.

7. Blackman, *Seasons of Her Life: A Biography of Madeleine K. Albright*, p.106.

8. Dobbs, *Madeleine Albright: A Twentieth-Century Odyssey*, p. 143.

9. Byman, *Madam Secretary: The Story of Madeleine Albright*, p. 26.

10. Julia Reed, "Woman of the World." *Vogue*, September 1997, p. 644.

11. Ed Bradley, "Interview with Madeleine Albright." *Sixty Minutes.* CBS, February 9, 1997.

12. Blackman, *Seasons of Her Life: A Biography of Madeleine K. Albright*, p. 108.

13. Ibid., p. 113.

14. Susan Baer, "A Passion for Foreign Policy." *Baltimore Sun*, January 5, 1997, p. A9.

15. Dobbs, *Madeleine Albright: A Twentieth-Century Odyssey*, p. 153.

CHAPTER 6

1. Blood, *Madam Secretary: A Biography of Madeleine Albright*, p. 75.

2. Dobbs, *Madeleine Albright: A Twentieth-Century Odyssey*, p.185.

3. Blackman, *Seasons of Her Life: A Biography of Madeleine K. Albright*, p. 129.

4. Ibid., p. 131.

5. Reed, "Woman of the World," p. 641.

6. Blackman, *Seasons of Her Life: A Biography of Madeleine K. Albright*, p.136.

7. Blood, *Madam Secretary: A Biography of Madeleine Albright*, p. 78.

8. Dobbs, *Madeleine Albright: A Twentieth-Century Odyssey*, p. 206.

9. Blackman, *Seasons of Her Life: A Biography of Madeleine K. Albright*, p. 15.

10. Ibid., p. 150.

CHAPTER 7

1. Blackman, *Seasons of Her Life: A Biography of Madeleine K. Albright*, p. 152.

2. Reed, "Woman of the World," p. 644.

3. Byman, *Madam Secretary: The Story of Madeleine Albright*, p. 38.

4. Ibid.

5. Sinclair, "Woman on Top of the World," p. F4.

6. Judy L. Hasday, *Madeleine Albright*, p. 84.

7. Blackman, *Seasons of Her Life: A Biography of Madeleine K. Albright*, p. 161.

8. Dobbs and Goshko, "Albright's Personal Odyssey Shaped Foreign Policy Beliefs," p. A25.

9. Blackman, *Seasons of Her Life: A Biography of Madeleine K. Albright*, p. 165.

10. Dobbs, *Madeleine Albright: A Twentieth-Century Odyssey*, p. 268.

11. Byman, *Madam Secretary: The Story of Madeleine Albright*, p. 42.

Notes

12. Ibid.

13. Ibid.

14. Elaine Sciolino, "Madeleine Albright's Audition." *The New York Times Magazine,* September 22, 1996, p. 104.

15. Blackman, *Seasons of Her Life: A Biography of Madeleine K. Albright,* p. 188.

16. Dobbs, *Madeleine Albright: A Twentieth-Century Odyssey,* p. 292.

17. Bradley, "Interview with Madeleine Albright."

CHAPTER 8

1. Baer, "A Passion for Foreign Policy," p. A9.

2. Blackman, *Seasons of Her Life: A Biography of Madeleine K. Albright,* p.192.

3. Geraldine Baum, "A Diplomatic Core." *Los Angeles Times,* February 8, 1995, p. F11.

4. Blood, *Madam Secretary: A Biography of Madeleine Albright,* p. 61.

5. Dobbs, *Madeleine Albright: A Twentieth-Century Odyssey,* p. 318.

6. Geraldine Ferraro, *Ferraro: My Story.* New York: Bantam Books, p. 118.

7. Jacob Heilbrunn, "Albright's Mission." *The New Republic,* August 22, 1994, p. 24.

8. Dobbs, *Madeleine Albright: A Twentieth-Century Odyssey,* p. 332.

9. Blood, *Madam Secretary: A Biography of Madeleine Albright,* p. 43.

10. Dan Balz, "UN Post Will Complete Odyssey for Albright: Daughter of Czech Diplomat Has Both Academic and Campaign Credentials." *The Washington Post,* December 23, 1992, p. A10.

CHAPTER 9

1. Baum, "A Diplomatic Core," p. F10.

2. Kevin Fedarko, "Clinton's Blunt Instrument." *Time,* October 31, 1994, p. 31.

3. Ibid.

4. Blackman, *Seasons of Her Life: A Biography of Madeleine K. Albright,* p. 245.

5. Nancy Gibbs, "Voice of America." *Time,* December 16, 1996, p. 33.

6. Blood, *Madam Secretary: A Biography of Madeleine Albright,* p. 100.

7. Ibid.

8. Baum, "A Diplomatic Core," p. F10.

9. Gibbs, "The Many Lives of Madeleine," p. 56.

10. Byman, *Madam Secretary: The Story of Madeleine Albright,* p. 61.

11. Blackman, *Seasons of Her Life: A Biography of Madeleine K. Albright,* p. 247.

12. Reed, "Woman of the World," p. 644.

13. Blackman, *Seasons of Her Life: A Biography of Madeleine K. Albright,* p. 247.

14. Byman, *Madam Secretary: The Story of Madeleine Albright,* p. 61.

15. Colin Powell, *My American Journey.* New York: Ballantine Books, 1995, p. 501.

16. Blood, *Madam Secretary: A Biography of Madeleine Albright*, p. 140.

17. Barbara Walters, "Interview with Madeleine Albright," *The Ten Most Fascinating People of 1997.* ABC, December 2, 1997.

18. Heilbrunn, "Albright's Mission," p. 26.

19. Carol Rosenberg, "Everybody Loves Tough Albright." *Miami Herald*, March 22, 1996, p. A1.

CHAPTER 10

1. "Albright Nominated As Secretary of State." CNN.com, December 5, 1996. <*http://www.cnn.com/US/9612/05/national.security/index.html*>.

2. Blackman, *Seasons of Her Life: A Biography of Madeleine K. Albright*, p. 279.

3. Weymouth, "'As I Find Out More, I'm Very Proud': An Exclusive Interview with Madeleine Albright," p. 30.

4. Blackman, *Seasons of Her Life: A Biography of Madeleine K. Albright*, p. 281.

5. Dobbs and Goshko, "Albright's Personal Odyssey Shaped Foreign Policy Beliefs," p. A64.

6. Blackman, *Seasons of Her Life: A Biography of Madeleine K. Albright*, p. 293.

7. Ibid., p. 302.

8. Ibid.

9. Blood, *Madam Secretary: A Biography of Madeleine Albright*, p.113.

10. Melinda Liu and Joseph Contreras, "Playing to the Crowd." *Newsweek*, September 22, 1997, p. 46.

11. Gibbs, "The Many Lives of Madeleine," p. 56.

12. Hasday, *Madeleine Albright*, p. 124.

Bibliography

Albright, Madeleine. "Message from the Secretary of State." *The Mini Page*, March 17, 1996, p. 4.

Baer, Susan. "A Passion for Foreign Policy." *Baltimore Sun*, January 5, 1997, sec. A.

Balz, Dan. "UN Post Will Complete Odyssey for Albright: Daughter of Czech Diplomat Has Both Academic and Campaign Credentials." *The Washington Post*, December 23, 1992, sec. A.

Baum, Geraldine. "A Diplomatic Core." *Los Angeles Times*, February 8, 1995, sec. F.

Blackman, Ann. *Seasons of Her Life: A Biography of Madeleine Korbel Albright*. New York: Scribner, 1998.

Blood, Thomas. *Madam Secretary: A Biography of Madeleine Albright*. New York: St. Martin's Press, 1997.

Bradley, Ed. Interview with Madeleine Albright. *Sixty Minutes*, CBS, February 9, 1997.

Byman, Jeremy. *Madam Secretary: The Story of Madeleine Albright*. Greensboro, N.C.: Morgan Reynolds, 1998.

Dobbs, Michael. *Madeline Albright: A Twentieth-Century Odyssey*. New York: Henry Holt, 1999.

Dobbs, Michael, and John M. Goshko. "Albright's Personal Odyssey Shaped Foreign Policy Beliefs." *Washington Post*, December 6, 1996, sec. A.

Fedarko, Kevin. "Clinton's Blunt Instrument." *Time*, October 31, 1994.

Ferraro, Geraldine. *Ferraro: My Story*. New York: Bantam Books, 1985.

Gibbs, Nancy. "The Many Lives of Madeleine." *Time*, February 17, 1997.

———. "The Voice of America." *Time*, December 16, 1996.

Hasday, Judy L. *Madeleine Albright*. New York: Chelsea House, 1999.

Heilbrunn, Jacob. "Albright's Mission." *The New Republic*, August 22 and 29, 1994.

"Kim's Nuclear Gamble." Interview with Madeleine Albright. *Frontline*, PBS. March 27, 2003.

King, Larry. Interview with Madeleine K. Albright. *Larry King Live*, CNN, January 24, 1997.

Liu, Melinda, and Joseph Contreras. "Playing to the Crowd." *Newsweek*, September 22, 1997.

Powell, Colin. *My American Journey*. New York: Ballantine Books, 1995.

Reed, Julia. "Woman of the World." *Vogue*, September 1997.

Rosenberg, Carol. "Everybody Loves Tough Albright." *Miami Herald,* March 22, 1996, sec. A.

Sciolino, Elaine. "Madeleine Albright's Audition." *The New York Times Magazine,* September 22, 1996.

Sinclair, Molly. "Woman On Top of the World." *Washington Post,* January 6, 1991, sec. F.

Walters, Barbara. Interview with Madeleine Albright. *The Ten Most Fascinating People of 1997.* ABC, December 2, 1997.

Weymouth, Lally. " 'As I Find Out More, I'm Very Proud': An Exclusive Interview with Madeleine Albright." *Newsweek,* February 24, 1997.

Websites

"Albright Nominated as Secretary of State." *CNN Interactive,* December 5, 1996. http://www.cnn.com/US/9612/05/national.security/index.html

"US Sends Mixed Message to UN." *CBS NEWS.com,* December 13, 1999. http://www.cbsnews.com

Further Reading

Books

Albright, Madeleine. *Madam Secretary.* New York: Miramax Books, 2003.

Blackman, Ann. *Seasons of Her Life: A Biography of Madeleine Korbel Albright.* New York: Scribner, 1998.

Byman, Jeremy. *Madam Secretary: The Story of Madeleine Albright.* Greensboro, N.C.: Morgan Reynolds, 1998.

Dobbs, Michael. *Madeline Albright: A Twentieth-Century Odyssey.* New York: Henry Holt, 1999.

Hasday, Judy L. *Women of Achievement: Madeleine Albright.* Philadelphia: Chelsea House, 1999.

Websites
The Albright Group, LLC
http://www.thealbrightgroupllc.com

Pew Research Center: For the People and the Press
http://people-press.com

Woodrow Wilson International Center for Scholars
http://wwics.si.edu

Index

Index

Credits

page:

3:   Courtesy U.S. Department of State

13: Courtesy U.S. Department of State

23: Courtesy U.S. Department of State

34: Courtesy U.S. Department of State

49: Courtesy U.S. Department of State

54: Courtesy U.S. Department of State

60: Courtesy U.S. Department of State

Cover: Courtesy U.S. Deparment of State

74: © Najlah Feanny/CORBIS SABA

78: © MARKOWITZ JEFFREY/CORBIS SYGMA

82: Courtesy U.S. Department of State

91: Courtesy U.S. Department of State

101: Associated Press, AP/Ronald Zak

About the Author

Kerry Acker is a freelance writer and editor based in Brooklyn, New York. Some of her other books for young adults include *Jimmy Carter* and *Gerhard Schroeder* in Chelsea House's MAJOR WORLD LEADERS series, and *Dorothea Lange* and *Nina Simone* in the WOMEN IN THE ARTS series.